The Accidental Salesperson

The Accidental Salesperson

The Handbook for Selling Like a Professional in Everyday Life

Allan Barmak

iUniverse, Inc.
New York Lincoln Shanghai

The Accidental Salesperson
The Handbook for Selling Like a Professional in Everyday Life

iUniverse books may be ordered through booksellers or by contacting:

iUniverse
2021 Pine Lake Road, Suite 100
Lincoln, NE 68512
www.iuniverse.com
1-800-Authors (1-800-288-4677)

www.theaccidentalsalesperson.com

ISBN: 978-0-595-45277-4 (pbk)
ISBN: 978-0-595-69377-1 (cloth)
ISBN: 978-0-595-89592-2 (ebk)

Printed in the United States of America

Contents

Acknowledgments vii

Introduction 1

1. Understanding Your Sales Prospect 7

2. Preparation Leads to Sales Success 19

3. Initiating the Sales Process 33

4. Trackability and Accountability 41

5. During the Sale 47

6. The Heart of the Sales Interaction: The Presentation 63

7. The Salesperson's Worst Fear: Objections 79

8. People Hate to Say "No" 87

9. Negotiation 91

10. After the "No" or After the Sale 103

Conclusion 115

Keep in Touch! 119

Acknowledgments

I would like to thank everyone who has helped me put this book together. Thank you to Mark Dewey who took a chance and gave a big-time sales job to a kid out of college. Thank you to Arden Colace for keeping me on the path of a sales career.

Thank you to my kids, for allowing me to practice my accidental sales techniques on them, whether they knew it or not. Finally, thank you to my wife Julie, for continuing to encourage me to stick with what I'm good at.

Introduction

What is a salesperson? Just the mention of the word evokes images of a guy with slicked-back hair in a cheap suit, with a sly grin, looking for his first chance to take your money. Salespeople are parodied, ignored, and are often looked down upon. But we are all salespeople, whether by design or by accident. Regardless of your place in the organizational chart of your business and regardless of your typical responsibilities around the office, or at home, or wherever you are, you're a salesperson. You started at a young age when you tried to negotiate with your parents for a later bedtime, and you are still selling today. Did you ever trade baseball cards when you were a kid? That's sales. Did you ever negotiate with your friends as to which clothes Barbie got to wear? That's sales, and you've been a salesperson for a long time.

When a salesperson cold-calls your home or office, your first reaction is probably to hang up on him or her. I'm guilty of this too. When I get a call at home, I check the caller-ID. If the number comes up as "unavailable," I usually think to myself, "Ignore the phone, it's probably just a salesperson."

I'll admit that when I was in high school and in college, I didn't aspire to be a Professional Salesperson. Nobody does. I think I wanted to be a lawyer because I liked to debate. Even during my senior year of college, I wanted to be a computer programmer, since those were the hot jobs at the time. It was because of this goal that I accidentally started my sales career. I had an internship that year and my boss knew someone who worked at America Online. I didn't know much about the company, but I knew that it involved computers, so I thought that they might need computer programmers. I called my boss' friend every week for five months, asking if a computer programming job had opened up.

Every week he said "no," until one day he called me back. I'll always remember what he told me:

1

"I still don't have any computer programming jobs for you, but you're persistent and polite. Do you know what you'd be good at? Sales."

His division was just starting an inside sales team, and he thought I'd be a good fit. Once I decided to give it a try, I learned something about myself—I love being a Professional Salesperson. I love the fact that I have a job where my performance can be tangibly tracked. I love that I can give myself a pay raise just by selling something. I love the competition between me and my peers. I love getting out into the field and debating with people as to why my product or service is good for them. Let me rephrase that in business language—I like talking and *negotiating* with people.

How did I accomplish the successful sales pitch and get my first official sales job? The same way that every Accidental Salesperson can do it—through common sense. Everyone has the skills needed to succeed in sales, it's just that we all need help learning how to identify a sales situation so we can apply those skills appropriately.

You've been a salesperson as a parent. You've been a salesperson as a student in school. You've been a salesperson as you tried to talk your way out of a traffic ticket. It may not say it on your business card, you may not even *have* a business card, but regardless, you are a salesperson.

Speaking of business cards, have you ever noticed that it is rare to find someone who carries a card that simply says "salesperson?" People are so embarrassed by the stigma of being called a salesperson that they will come up with any title to try to hide their true profession. I just took a look through the pile of business cards I have on my desk now, and here are some of the titles listed:

- Business Development Director
- Procurement Agent
- Vice-President of Business Development (I actually know three different VPs of Business Development within this particular company)
- Partnership Director
- Senior Account Executive
- Contracting Director

My personal favorite is the *Contracting Director*. What exactly does a Contracting Director do? I found out the detailed job description by talking to this person. As it turns out, he is in charge of bringing new contracts into the business. In other words, he's responsible for letting people know about what his business can offer, and then getting them to sign a contract for those products or services. This is where the title of *Contracting Director* comes from. In the end, he's responsible for closing contracts and thus, making sales. He's a salesperson in every sense of the word.

Before you can truly benefit from learning the skills of the Professional Salesperson, you need to get over the negativity that's often associated with that label. Don't be ashamed of acting like a salesperson to someone. Even the Accidental Salesperson typically feels a little uncomfortable when he realizes he used something that may have been perceived as a sales trick to get something he wanted.

There are no tricks in successful sales interactions. A sale is the result of two parties reaching a mutually beneficial agreement. Even if you are a Managing Partner of a law firm, and you have ever told one person about what you do, you're a salesperson. In that case, you may not have been recruiting potential clients at that exact moment, but I'm sure you put a spin on your job description which talked about the benefits of working with your firm. What about the doctor who is trying to convince his colleagues that a new surgical procedure could benefit a patient? He'll need to give a pretty good sales pitch in order to get his point across. Maybe you are a Human Resources Manager, responsible for interviewing new hires. You're still a salesperson. Part of your job is to get the applicant pool excited about the opportunity to work for your company.

Even if you're a full-time homemaker, and you've ever been faced with the task of getting your kids to finish their dinner, you've been a salesperson. Think about it—in that basic interaction of getting your son or daughter to finish the food on his or her plate, you have gone through most of the stages of the sales process which I'll talk about later in this book:

1. Identify your potential sales target (your child)
2. Engage in dialogue to learn more about your prospect (trying to figure out why they won't eat their green beans … this is a stage which I'll later call the "needs analysis")
3. Negotiate (offer dessert in exchange for eating the meal, or threaten to send them to bed early if they don't)
4. Close the deal

Throughout this book, I will highlight the ways that the Professional Salesperson conducts his sales activities, and then I will interject examples of how everyone, as the Accidental Salesperson, can apply those tips and techniques in their daily lives. You will find that regardless of whether or not you are a Professional Salesperson or Accidental Salesperson, the fundamentals of sales interactions can be applied to any situation. Sales is a great job—the Professional Salesperson is part of a team responsible for bringing assets, in the form of revenue, intellectual talent, or other resources, into the business through sales, or by brokering win-win partnerships that can help the business. My hope is that you, as the Accidental Salesperson, will be able to learn from the experience of the Professional Salesperson.

The foundation of this book is that sales is a part of most everyday interactions. Think about what defines a salesperson, and think how it applies to the father of a household, for example. In this case, the business unit is the family. Let's say that the father is looking to hire a painter to paint a room in his house. He will initiate contact with the painter, and he may also negotiate the price of the job. These are two sales activities that will result in the salesperson (the father) bringing an asset (a painter who can paint the house) into the business (the family unit). The result of this sales interaction is a win-win partnership—the painter will get paid for the job, and the business will get something that they wanted, a painted room.

Sales is the backbone of every kind of interaction; it has a role in each and every individual business function that any office conducts, or anything you may do personally.

You can walk into any bookstore and find thousands of different books that offer advice as to <u>how</u> to sell regardless of what industry you work in, or whatever your business does on a daily basis. Each of these books is an educational tool, and like any kind of educational tool, each offers different bits of information, or tips and pointers that can help you achieve success. Personally, I like to read different sales books as often as possible. I usually find it helpful to have the goal of trying to get several pieces of information from each book and then adopting just a few of the things that I learned. It is next to impossible to implement all the information that is contained within any given book. The fact is that certain things work for certain people and different things work for other people. To that end, this book does not intend to be the definitive resource for all sales. I don't claim to offer the magic key that will lead to unlimited success in the world of sales whether you are a Professional or Accidental Salesperson. This book should be used as a reference that you, the salesperson, regardless of your official title, can adapt to your specific sales interactions.

My goal is to offer a strong foundation that will help you achieve success in the long run. I have organized this book by highlighting the different aspects of a sales transaction from start to finish, including all things in between. Read through the whole book one time and then go back and pick out the chapters which are most relevant for you.

The Accidental Salesperson is most successful when he sells based on common sense, with a little help from understanding the foundations highlighted by the Professional Salesperson. Most of the tips and techniques in this book aren't groundbreaking. They are just a compilation of ideas that will help increase your chances of finishing on the successful side of your sales interactions. Whether you are a salesperson by occupation or a salesperson by accidental circumstance, you will be able to learn from this book.

Understanding Your Sales Prospect

Every person is a business owner. They might not run a big company that is traded on the New York Stock Exchange, they might not even own a sole proprietorship, but they own a business. Each person's day-to-day life is his business. Think about it in the traditional sense—what does a business do? Typically, a business offers a product or service to the general public. The business conducts many different functions—they have revenue coming into the business, typically earned from the product or service they offer, they buy office supplies, they pay rent on their office space, and they keep track of their finances. In this regard, doesn't the homemaker conduct the same general functions as a CEO?

- He or she is running the business of the house.
- The business of the family unit has a revenue stream of income in the form of salary earned by the husband and/or the wife.
- The family pays rent on their office space, probably in the form of a monthly mortgage.
- The homemaker keeps track of their finances, probably in the form of a personal budget so that he knows what the expenses are for office upkeep. The *office upkeep* could be clothes for the kids, electricity for the house, etc.

The first step to any sales approach is to know the prospect. Each business a Professional Salesperson targets is composed of people who work to keep that business moving forward. Of course, all people are unique, and the people who work at a business, or in a business unit, make that business unique. As a result, each sales approach should also be unique.

Even though all people are different, there are three facts which are common to almost everyone you would interact with:

> 1) **People have unique strengths and weaknesses**. They will respect the opinion of someone who is more skilled or knowledgeable in an area where they themselves are weaker.
>
> 2) **People will stretch themselves thin if they don't have a better option.** Even though a professional or specialist could help things run more efficiently.
>
> 3) **People buy from those they know, like, and TRUST**.

If you can understand these issues, you will position yourself to achieve success selling where both your competition and your peers fail. Let's take a look at each of these issues in turn.

Fact #1: People Have Unique Strengths and Weaknesses

Any business unit, regardless of size, even down to the level of an individual, is challenged with trying to focus on what they do best. Focusing on what you do best results in maximum efficiency. Look at any sports team. The players are arranged so that they are focusing on what they do best. On a football team, for example, the quarterback will be able to do his best for the team if he is actually leading the offense, handing off the ball and passing it. If, for example, the place kicker was trying to play the quarterback's position, he wouldn't be putting his best food forward, so to speak. The same is true in the business world. In order to succeed, businesses need to focus on the things that they know how to do best—their **core competencies**.

One of the things which makes each business unique is that it has a limited range of expertise. The expertise of the business as a whole is innately connected to the expertise of its individual employees. If, for example, you consider a ten-person law firm, chances are that those ten lawyers and assistants know a lot about law, more so than they know about marketing, or even technology. Law is their *core competency*. The Professional Salesperson will offer value to those prospects by showing how whatever he is pitching will allow each of the lawyers to focus on his core competency, and thus work more efficiently and effectively overall.

Anyone, in or out of the business world, wants to work more efficiently and effectively. Think about this in terms of the Accidental Salesperson. If you were a small business owner, or even a full-time homemaker, and someone approached you with a way that your life, or business, could become more efficient and effective, you would at least listen. For a business, an increase in efficiency leads to an increase in productivity which leads to an increase in revenue. This means the business makes more money, which is, of course, the end goal of any company, big or small. That's why the employees are there—to keep money coming in.

When it comes right down to it, it is very hard to find someone who is truly working for the love of the job. There is usually some kind of financial motivation. This is not to say it is impossible to find a job you love. I love being a salesperson, but as a whole, people are in business to make money. Companies are in business to make money. People, as an individual business unit, live their lives trying to make more money and accumulate greater wealth. If the salesperson can show a way that his prospect can make more money or save more money, then the sales pitch is worth listening to. Many successful sales interactions can be boiled down to the need for efficiency in the wake of people having unique strengths and weaknesses.

From the business perspective, a great example of the connection between efficiency and the focus on core competencies can be found in the beginnings of the American Industrial Revolution. In the early 1900s, Henry Ford came up with the idea of mass production to help his company build automobiles more efficiently and effectively. In general, the way it worked was that individual laborers stayed in place along an assembly line conveyor belt. As the parts moved by, each worker would assemble his specific widget and then put the completed piece back on the belt so that the next person down the line could make their own modifications or additions. Eventually, the completed product took shape. The benefit of this arrangement was that each person was only responsible for his specific function. Each person focused on what he did best. For example, one person was responsible for putting the wheel axle together, while another person was responsible for building just one part of the engine.

The reason the initial concept of mass production worked so well was because it allowed a person to focus on only one task, which became his core competency. Each worker became extremely skilled in performing his specific task because of the repetitiveness and consistency of the job. This allowed each individual worker to maximize his own productivity, since he would learn how to get his personal job done most efficiently. This would, in turn, maximize the productivity of the entire company. The bottom line is that if people focus on their core competencies, they will become more efficient, and of course, efficiency is better than waste.

This is an obvious truth, but one that can easily be forgotten by the Accidental Salesperson.

The simple fact that efficiency is worth paying for can be used to sell even the most basic household product. Let's look at the professional vacuum cleaner salesman—his pitch is that his vacuum cleaner picks up dirt faster and more thoroughly than anything else, so that the homemaker spends less time actually cleaning the house. This allows the homemaker to have more time to do other things. It's all about efficiency.

To illustrate the benefits of allowing a business to focus on its core competencies, let's again look at a Professional Salesperson trying to sell to that same ten-person law firm I talked about earlier. Let's pretend the salesperson is selling an advertising program to the firm. Some of the things he might highlight as he was pitching the prospect are that his core competency is advertising—it's what he knows best. He will let the prospect know that he has made a career out of helping businesses reach a specific target demographic and achieve success through advertising. Most importantly, he will highlight the extensive research that has to be done in order to get the advertising message in front of the right audience.

Especially if the Professional Salesperson is selling to a service firm that bills by the hour, like the law firm in this example, he may find it useful to list his benefits to that firm in financial terms. In other words, after he explains to the firm the hours of research that his company does in order to match buyers with sellers, he will lay out the alternative. He may ask them:

"The reason our advertising agency has been able to deliver so much success to our clients is because we complete hours of market research to make sure that we get you in front of the right audience. As a lawyer billing $300 an hour, if you were to just spend three hours doing the necessary marketing research instead of us, it would cost you almost $1,000 in lost billing time. *Wouldn't it be more efficient if my company focused on the marketing plan?* Not only will you increase the odds of this program succeeding, but we will all be focusing on what we do best—we'll take care of the marketing while you practice law."

In the end, regardless of the exact words he uses and regardless of who he is pitching to, **the key is to highlight increased efficiency and effectiveness through the focus on core competencies**. In other words, if the prospect allows the salesperson to do what he does best, the prospect will have more time to do what he does best. Trying to stay on task through focusing on their core competencies is something that everyone struggles with every day. The salesperson who can help get the prospect on track has an advantage in making the sale.

Fact #2: People Will Stretch Themselves Thin if They Don't Have a Better Option

With any grouping of people, whether in business, sports, or anything else, the bigger the group, the more potential resources that group has. If you follow sports, you may know that regardless of the sport, the championship teams are almost always considered to have greater *depth* than their competitors. Even in an individual sport, such as golf, championship players typically have a greater depth of resources. Tiger Woods continues to win majors because he has a greater repertoire of shots to choose from when he is in trouble on the course. More shots to choose from means a greater chance of making the shot which will get him closer to his goal of getting the ball in the cup.

Consider the sport of basketball, where there are five players on each team who can participate in the game at any given time. If this basketball team had depth it would mean that more players can come off the bench as the starting five fatigued. In football, depth may mean that the team has a great back-up quarterback ready to come in if the starting quarterback gets injured. Whether in sports or in business, it all comes down to resources—the more people that a business unit has at its disposal, the easier it is for them to withstand any period of trouble without disrupting the flow of the organization. However, along those lines, if a business doesn't have the exact resources it needs, it will be forced to make the most out of the resources it does have.

Going back to the football example, if a team with depth, meaning that it has a good supply of alternative players who can do the job, loses its starting quarterback to injury, a qualified, skilled, back-up quarterback can enter the game without necessitating a complete overhaul of the gameplan. On a team without as much depth, if the starting quarterback gets hurt, they may have to look to a free agent or someone outside of the team in order to fill the vacancy with a player who has as much competency as the original starting quarterback. If that were the case, there would be extensive disruption to the team in the sense that it would now have a new player who has to learn the offense, blend in with new teammates, etc. This not only causes delays, but will probably cause the team to suffer in the short-term.

> It all comes down to *resources*.

In business, if a company has deep resources, not only can it withstand the typical ebb and flow of the business world with minimal disruption, but it also has more people to call on when a job needs to get done. For example, it is possible that the Accounting Department and Marketing Department of a larger corporation could consist of hundreds of people each. That equates to hundreds of brains that can be accessible to help resolve any issue which may come up. It also means that that huge brain power can be used to help the company move ahead strategically. In a 100-person Accounting Department, if one person is out sick for a day or two, the company will not skip a beat. On the other hand, if you were to look at a five-person small business, it might have one person serving both functions of Marketing and Accounting. If that person goes out sick, the marketing and accounting functions will be put on hold for a couple of days.

Think about the importance of resources in the family unit—if Mom is out sick for a day, think of how that business unit suffers. Who will be able to make the lunches for the kids? Who can get them ready for school? The family unit is a prototypical small business that is always stretched thin with regard to resources. Think about this through your sales interactions. If you were to offer a solution to your prospect which could help alleviate the fact that they are stretched thin, you will probably get yourself closer to making the sale.

Small businesses, even individuals you interact with everyday, are often forced to use their limited resources for multiple functions. This means that small changes anywhere within the organizational structure of the business can have a ripple effect. When considering this fact, a Professional Salesperson often highlights how his or her product or service can help alleviate or replace some of the necessary tasks or operations common to a small business unit so that the limited resources are freed-up for other things. Regardless of who he sells to, the same rules still apply—he would still highlight the potential efficiencies in his sales solution. Maybe the salesperson is pitching a maid service to a homemaker. A successful sales pitch would probably show how allowing professionals to clean the house would free the homemaker, who is the prospect in this case, to do other things.

The pitch would be, "If you let me clean your home, you'll have two extra hours a week to spend with your children."

What if you were the one being pitched to? Wouldn't you consider paying the maid service to free up some of you resources, like your time?

Going back to the earlier discussion of core competencies, we can see that because small businesses and individuals are forced to designate multiple tasks to their limited resources, it is likely that they are being pulled away from their core competencies. The common sense approach of the Accidental Salesperson will show how his offer can help free-up resources and allow people to focus on what they do best. One thing to remember as an Accidental Salesperson is that **it is always a good idea to angle your sales pitch to highlight how your solution leads to increased efficiency and effectiveness.**

Every sales situation is centered on some need for increased efficiency or effectiveness. Even down to a basic sale, there is still this focus. For example, why did you buy a vacuum cleaner for your house? It's probably because you realized that it is more efficient to use a machine to pick up dust and dirt rather than for you to do it by hand. The vacuum cleaner salesperson, or the vacuum cleaner store, made the sale based on the innate increased efficiencies his product could deliver.

Fact #3: People buy from those they know, like, and TRUST

The Professional Salesperson knows that trust and relationship-building are extremely important. In the business world, and even in someone's personal life, there is a natural inclination to resist change. The status quo is much safer than the uncertainty of something that has never been done before. Any outside influence threatens a certain level of stability that had been built up in that business unit. If that business unit is a family, there are many examples of how an outside influence can affect the balance of that organization. Pretend that a decision is made to have a personal chef cook dinner for the family in order to free-up some of Mom or Dad's time. What is the ripple effect of this seemingly inconsequential change?

- What if the family doesn't like the new dinners that are cooked?
- What will Mom and Dad do with their extra free time?
- How will the cost of the chef affect the family's monthly budget?

In order to gently move people away from the perception of security from the status quo, **the salesperson needs to establish trust**. In this example, even the chef pitching his services is a salesperson. He would need to talk about the benefits of his service by answering the family's concerns. Maybe he offers to cook them a free meal so they can taste the food, answering objection #1. Maybe he shows how his services really aren't that expensive, answering objection #3. There are many different things he could do. For any salesperson, building trust with the prospect will make for a smoother, and often more successful, sales experience.

Many times, people fail to accept a sales proposal because of the threat of negative consequences if they move off of the status quo. Because the fear of the unknown is pervasive in all business decisions and interactions, decision makers place a high value on trust and relationship-building. We have already talked about the fact that smaller organizations are typically stretched thin when it comes to resources, and because of this, when a need arises, it is important for that business to partner with a company, or a person, who has expertise in a field outside of their own core competencies, so that they can be more efficient. This change doesn't happen overnight. The Professional Salesperson knows that he must first focus on earning a prospect's trust before he can earn their business.

A common rule of sales is that people buy from who they know and like. Sales exchanges between friends are typically more successful than sales exchanges between adversaries. When the decision-maker of a business, whether it is the managing partner of a professional service firm, or the head of a household, agrees to the conditions of a sale with a salesperson, he is agreeing to integrate that product or service into the day-to-day life of his organization. The product or service that the salesperson is offering is going to have a ripple effect throughout the whole business unit. Before someone makes a decision to accept a new asset into their infrastructure, they first need to have built trust in the salesperson who was pitching them. Even when the salesperson is selling to families, the product or service he is selling affects that "company," or family unit. Here's another example—what if a family was buying a new minivan? For the sake of the family, reliability is probably a big concern. Before they make that purchase, the family needs to trust that the car salesperson is giving them accurate information regarding the car they are looking to buy.

Trust and relationship-building are held in high regard by any sales prospect who cannot afford wild swings in his or her environment. Many times, the vendor evaluation process of a small business or individual is as stringent as the internal hiring process of a big company. Think of this in common sense terms—obviously, you would rather spend time with people you know and like. As an

Accidental Salesperson, take this with you into all of your sales interactions and get the prospect to like you. Focus on selling yourself like you would during a personal job interview. If you build a strong foundation through relationships and trust, you will have a solid platform for future sales success. **The most successful and efficient sales interactions are between people who know, like, and trust each other.**

The Accidental Salesperson Interacting With a Small Business

Throughout this book, I will give examples of how people who don't consider themselves salespeople can achieve sales success. That's the whole concept of the Accidental Salesperson—**sales are a part of everything you do in life, and if you can arm yourself with basic sales skills, you'll achieve greater success**. Here is the first example:

John has an interview with a small trade association for a job as a financial officer. Before going into the interview, John realizes that even though the specific position he is seeking does not have a sales function, he's going to need to use sales skills to get the job. The association he is interviewing with is a classic small business. It displays the same three factors that are common in all sales interactions—the prospect wants to focus on what they do best, the prospect is stretching himself thin, and he is looking for an expert to trust. John will use this knowledge to show how he is the right person for the job.

As an Accidental Salesperson, there's no need for John to worry about remembering sales tricks. There are no tricks. All he needs in order to be successful is the ability to break the situation down into the different elements of a sales interaction:

1. There is a salesperson and a prospect
2. The prospect has specific needs
3. The salesperson's goal is to show the prospect how he can meet those specific needs

Everything else that happens throughout the process is simply peripheral to those three elements of a sales interaction.

In this case, here's how those elements lay out:

Salesperson: John

Prospect: Small Trade Association

Prospect's Need: Financial Officer

The basic question is: can the salesperson meet the prospect's needs, and greatly increase his chances of making the sale?

Through his preliminary research, John realizes that the trade association he is targeting is stretched thin and has a strong desire to have other tasks and responsibilities taken care of. He also recognizes the value of trust and relationship-building to his prospect.

Obviously, most of the candidates John is competing with will only try to highlight their ability to meet the specific job description that they are interviewing for. In order to make himself stand out from the competition, John has done his research and noticed that the company is also looking for a marketing associate. Years ago, John had worked at an advertising agency. This is an asset which he can use to his advantage.

At the interview, John outlines how he is an exact match for each of the qualifications that have been highlighted in the job description, which allows him to show how he can help the business focus on core competencies. Then he takes the next step—he talks about his experience at the advertising agency, and how he would also work well with whomever they bring in as a marketing associate. He talks about how developing marketing ideas should be part of a collaborative effort, and how, since the trade association is hiring a new marketing employee, it would be important to have other people within the organization who also have some experience with marketing, showing an understanding of the business' need to have multiple uses of resources.

Now, all of a sudden, the HR Manager is realizing that by hiring John, not only will he be able to fill the vacancy for a financial associate, which is the primary expressed need, but after he fills the marketing vacancy, the business will have the components of a small marketing team. John, the Accidental Salesperson, has not only shown how what he is selling is more than a good match for the needs of his prospect, but he has also begun to build a good relationship with his prospect by demonstrating the extra effort he put in by researching the business ahead of time.

Preparation Leads to Sales Success

The Professional Salesperson has a unique job in the sense that the results of his efforts are tangible. He is tracked on the basis of closed sales, or number of calls, or any of a number of additional measures. Regardless of the industry the Professional Salesperson works in, there are tools that can help him perform better, and give himself an advantage over his peers.

The Professional Salesperson recognizes that preparation and planning are the keys to success in sales as in most anything he would ever do. This means preparation as to finding out who his prospects are, why they would want what he is selling, and what kind of obstacles may be in his way as he tries to make the sale. Before he starts out selling any product, whether he is selling to small or large businesses, the Professional Salesperson asks himself the basic question:

"Why would someone want to buy what I'm selling?"

This will get him thinking about the buying motives of the prospect, along with some of the features and advantages of his product. This common sense approach to a sales pitch is easily translated to the Accidental Salesperson, who, before he initiates any sales interaction, should ask himself that same question. If the question cannot be answered, it may mean that the salesperson should consider possible changes to what he is selling in order to make it more appealing to the target audience.

> The Professional Salesperson will try to highlight the following two elements of what he is selling—**features and advantages**. Here is the basic difference between the two:
>
> *Features* are black and white explanations of specific elements of the sales offering. These are tangible items.
>
> *Advantages* are a supplement to features, and explain how the sales offering can deliver a positive result to the prospect.

To give an example further explaining the difference between features and advantages, let's look at a car salesperson. Here are some *features* of the car that he is selling:

- V8 engine
- Alloy wheels
- In-dash CD changer
- Leather seats

Again, these are specific elements which are part of the car that no one can disagree with. In other words, the car either has leather seats or it doesn't. These features are not in all cars, just in the specific car that the salesman is talking about in this case.

Here are some *advantages* of the car that he is selling, which he can pitch to his prospect. Remember, these are *subjective* aspects of his specific product:

- Spend less time at the pump, because it gets great gas mileage
- Minimize huge unplanned expenses, because this car has a warranty that lasts for 40,000 more miles than the competition's, meaning that the customer won't have to worry about putting out a lot of money if the transmission goes out after the typical warranty period
- Protect your family, because this car offers state-of-the-art air bags and safety protection

As you can see, the main difference between features and advantages is that the features explain what is included in the car, and the advantages answer the question "what's in it for me?" Typically, and in this example, features are things common to other similar products. In this case, we're talking about cars. For example, it would be safe to assume that other automobiles in the class of the car we're talking about would generally have the same features. *Advantages* are what make the specific product stand out above any other alternatives.

For the Professional Salesperson, the more research he does on his potential prospects, the easier it will be for him to highlight advantages which are a direct match to their needs. If the salesperson has a specific pool of competitors who he runs across frequently, he may find it helpful to position his advantages to show

how his product stands out, specifically in contrast to his peers who are also trying to reach that same prospect. The bottom line is that **planning and research are keys to success in any sales situation.**

Taking the example one step further, let's look at everything from another point of view. Pretend you're at a party and you run into two different car salespeople. The first one, after learning you may be in the market to buy a car, says to you, "I've got the perfect car for you—it's got a V8 engine, alloy wheels, leather seats, and even an in-dash CD changer. Come by the dealership and I'll show you."

At this point, you're thinking "So what? I can name ten different cars that have the same thing. Why should I waste my time and go down to his dealership?"

So, you wander around the party a little more and you run into the second car salesperson. He learns you may be looking to buy a car and he tells you, "I've got the perfect car for you—you'll save money on gas, you won't have to worry about huge expenses on the car for a long time and you will even be able to keep your kids safer than they've ever been in an automobile. Come by the dealership and I'll show it to you."

Wouldn't the second salesperson's pitch at least get you interested to learn more about the car? If it were me in the same position, I would go down to the dealership to get more specifics. This is when I'll learn about the *features*. In this case, there's no reason for me not to go down and check things out. All of those advantages are appealing to me. I want to save money on gas, I don't want to worry about unplanned car expenses, and I want to keep my kids safe. At the very least, I'm intrigued as to how one car could have all those advantages for me. As this example shows, the more a salesperson knows about his target audience, the more likely he is to make the sale.

As an Accidental Salesperson, remember that in your world, just like the Professional Salesperson, preparation leads to success. Take the time to truly evaluate what you are trying to sell. Why would someone accept your proposal? How can your offering have a positive impact on your prospect? How can you position your product to be most appealing to your target audience? Most importantly, with consideration to the three commonalities between most sales prospects (focus on core competencies, multiple use of resources, importance of trust and relationship-building), is what you're offering a good fit?

Preparation in Creating the Value Proposition

When a salesperson sells to a specific prospect, it's not enough to list features and advantages, he needs to explain the *value* of the features and advantages as it pertains to the specific prospect's business. An important first step in sales success for the Professional Salesperson is learning the *value* of his product or service. The same is true for the Accidental Salesperson.

Before I go further, I need to get into an important definitional distinction between **value** and **price**, since **value** is different from **price** when talking about a product or service.

Price is how much something costs, and value is what it's worth.

Price is an objective measure, and value is innately *subjective*. For example, I love buying gadgets, and pretty much anything associated with the newest technology. When I wanted to get a surround-sound system for the family room, both my wife and I could agree on the price of the product, since it was tangibly printed on the box, but of course, we had differing views of the value. After we had everything installed, she swore that she couldn't tell the difference between the traditional sound coming from the TV and the sound from the new system. Of course, I was ecstatic with the sound quality. It was just that my wife and I had different views of value.

There's a joke that I once heard that really speaks to the importance of value: An old woman is walking by the bank of a river when she sees a frog sitting on a rock.

She looks down at the frog, and the frog looks back at her and says "Give me a kiss and I will give you more money than you ever dreamed of."

The woman looks down at the frog, picks it up, and shoves it into her pocket. She walks a little further and by this point, the frog has worked his head out of her pocket. He calls up to her again and says "Didn't you hear me? I'll give you millions of dollars; all you would need to do is give me a kiss." The woman shoved the frog deeper into her pocket.

Eventually, the frog popped out again and said. "I don't get it—just one kiss and you will be rich beyond your wildest dreams!" "Why won't you kiss me?"

The woman looked down at the frog and said, "At my age, I'd much rather have a talking frog."

This illustrates why, for the salesperson, preparation is key. Since *value* means different things to different people, the value proposition offered by the salesperson will need to be tweaked when addressing different businesses and different prospects. I've included a worksheet which will help you focus your efforts. If you know your target audience, you will be able to present a value proposition that will best resonate with your prospect's needs and goals.

The Value Proposition Worksheet

To help get you started with your value proposition, simply fill in the blanks and follow the next steps:

1) What company do you work for? _____

2) What are you pitching? _____

3) To whom? _____

4) What makes your sales offering unique? _____

5) Any success stories? _____

Now, just fill in the blanks in order to uncover your value proposition:

"Hi, I'm (NAME) from (ANSWER TO #1). We sell (POSITIVE ADJECTIVE) (ANSWER TO #2) to (ANSWER TO #3). The reason my [PRODUCT/ SERVICE] is unique is because (ANSWER TO #4). In fact, (ANSWER TO #5)."

The Value Proposition Worksheet

Now, I've filled in the worksheet, using an example of a clothing store:

1)	What company do you work for?	Great Clothes, LLC
2)	What are you selling?	High-end clothing (skirts, tops)
3)	Who is your target audience/best customer?	Women who want high fashion, but can't shop in NYC or Paris
4)	What makes your sales offering unique?	Our clothes have the "WOW" factor. An outfit that will look great on you, and you won't find it anywhere else.
5)	Any success stories?	Our clothes are so unique, we hear from our clients all the time that when they wear our clothes to a party, they always get plenty of compliments.

Now, just fill in the blanks:

Hi, I'm **Allan** from **Great Clothes**. We sell **high-end clothing to women who want high fashion, but can't shop in NYC or Paris**. The reason our **clothes** are unique is because **they have that "WOW" factor—an outfit that will look great on you, and you won't find it anywhere else**. In fact, **our clothes are so unique, we hear from our clients all the time that when they wear one of our dresses to a party, they always get plenty of compliments.**

The value proposition for interactions in the real world can be a little less formal. Pretend you are talking to a contractor who is pitching you on letting him wallpaper your kitchen. You want the contractor to lower his price. Although you are being sold to, you are also in the role of the Accidental Salesperson, and you can make a counter-sales pitch. You need a value proposition. Here it is:

"I was looking at the proposal for wallpapering the kitchen, and it's a little high. Would you be willing to cut your price by 10%? In exchange, I have two friends who are looking to decorate their houses, and I'll gladly give you their names. I referred the last contractor who was out here to finish our basement to my friends, and he ended up completing a $40,000 job for them."

Let's look at that value proposition for your proposal with consideration to the five questions we talked about earlier:

1. *What company do you work for?* This answer is implied, since your representing yourself
2. *What are you pitching?* A 10% discount off the original proposal
3. *To whom?* Implied, since you're selling to the contractor
4. *What makes your sales offering unique?* The wallpaper man might not get those valuable referrals from anyone else
5. *Any success stories?* The last referral turned into a $40,000 sale

As you can see, you can create a value proposition for anything that you are working on.

Preparation in Knowing the Decisonmaker

Now that you have a value proposition, who do you pitch it to? It's great to know the value of your sales offering, but you need to make sure your pitch is delivered to someone who can actually accept that sales proposal. Finding the right person to pitch to is one of the most difficult things a salesperson has to do, and it sometimes takes a good deal of preparation to get you to the right person. Who that decisionmaker is will vary from prospect to prospect, and business to business.

Even if you were a salesperson focused on pitching a much smaller business unit like the family, it is often difficult to find out who to pitch to because it is a challenge to determine specific roles. Is the wife responsible for the finances? Does the husband get the kids ready for school? Who cleans the house? Who cooks dinner? In the corporate world, large businesses have specific departments that are dedicated to specific business functions, so the Professional Salesperson's search for the ultimate decision maker will be much more linear. The salesperson who was calling on a large business and trying to sell advertising would most likely look to the Marketing Department. There, he will find a Marketing Director. The Marketing Directors of large companies have the responsibility of marketing the businesses. This means that part of their job description is to pick up the phone when a salesperson calls.

Traditionally, the mantra in sales is "go to the top." The Professional Salesperson knows that when selling to small businesses or individuals, this is not always true. In these scenarios, he will not necessarily focus on selling to the top—he will focus on selling to the person who will be making the ultimate decision on whether to buy his product or service.

In any kind of sales interactions, accidental or professional, remember to focus on finding the person who has the power to say "yes" or "no" to your sales pitch. The central point in this book is that we are all Accidental Salespeople and that the road to sales success starts with common sense. Along these lines, it doesn't matter who you are selling to, or what you are selling, but look to find the person who can approve your proposal. Why would you waste the time and effort you put into the sales pitch on someone who doesn't have the power to either make the final decision or even influence the final decision?

The Professional Salesperson will make sure everything he does leads up to a meeting with the person who can make a decision about his proposal. All of his research, all of his planning, is designed to get face-to-face with the ultimate decisionmaker. At times, the first contact in a business may not be the ultimate decision maker, but it might be someone who can get the salesperson closer to the person he needs. Remember when I talked earlier about the misconceptions related to the titles people have on their business card? The corporate title some-one goes by is, in reality, irrelevant to the Professional Salesperson. Especially if he is selling to an individual, that one person is the ultimate decisionmaker, even though his title is not CEO.

> Titles are never as important as *responsibilities* are.

The title of the person who makes the appropriate decisions for the Professional Salesperson will, in all likelihood, vary from business unit to business unit, and likewise, from prospect to prospect. It's not the title that someone has in an office that makes them a decision-maker; it's their job description or job responsibility. For example, many business decisions are made several levels below the CEO. This is because the CEO has other things to do. That's how he or she got to be CEO—by learning how to properly delegate their authority and disseminate tasks.

In every sales interaction, remember to focus your efforts on the person who can get you the sale.

Preparation through research

As an Accidental Salesperson, remember that people are comfortable with the status quo. We talked earlier about how people buy from others they know and like. One way to get someone to like you is to show that you know what you're talking about when it comes to whatever you're offering. Remember another thing I mentioned—people are always looking for those who can help them with something they can't do for themselves. Everyone respects an expert. It is not efficient for people or businesses to waste time doing things outside of their area of expertise. If you can show your prospect that you can be trusted with offering him advice, you'll be that much closer to making the sale, whatever that sales pitch may be.

Useful resources are all around you. The Professional Salesperson uses industry articles and other respected news sources to give himself and his sales offering credibility. He will typically have a set group of magazines or newspapers he looks at in order to keep up-to-date with issues, or other things that may affect his sales efforts or his prospects' businesses. Keeping up-to-date with what is going on around you is helpful for all salespeople, Accidental or Professional. The Accidental Salesperson, who simply scans through his local daily newspaper every morning, can learn a lot about what's going on around him.

> Knowledge is a key currency in the sales exchange—the more you know about the things you are pitching, the better off you will be. Learning about what is going on around you will help give you ideas as to how to build successful sales efforts.

Using an example from earlier, pretend you run a home cleaning service. You read in the paper that a new home builder has just bought land where he is going to put up fifty new homes. Naturally, people want their new homes to be clean, so now you have fifty new prospects for future business. Take the example one step further and use this knowledge to gain a competitive advantage over your peers. Every new home community has a model home where prospective home buyers take a tour. Why don't you approach the builder about cleaning the model home at a discount in exchange for putting a brochure for your business in that home so prospective home buyers can see it? Sometimes, all it takes is a little initiative and assertiveness. Either way, the more you know about your prospect as it pertains to what you are pitching, the better your chances of sales success.

Using the Internet as a Research Tool in your Preparation

The internet is the single most effective tool a Professional Salesperson uses to prepare to generate new business. Even the Accidental Salesperson can realize the benefits of the internet. Everything you need is one-click away on your computer. There are business databases, company websites with more information than their annual shareholder's report, and an unlimited amount of newspaper sites and news outlets. There's even plenty of local websites with information about what's going on in the community. However, all of that data might be overwhelming when you consider the volume of information that is available. As with everything else that has been covered in this book, the best way to make it manageable is to have a plan and focus on your particular niche. Take a step back. What is your sales objective? Figure out what websites are the most useful for you, and focus on the parts of those websites which provide the information that is most relevant for your sales efforts.

As an Accidental Salesperson, you should also take the time to check local websites. The major newspaper in your area should have a very extensive website, but often times, you can even find great information from the websites of the many smaller newspapers or community publications. In addition, depending on whom you are targeting as a sales prospect, local Chambers of Commerce are a great place to look. Most Chamber of Commerce websites not only have a complete searchable membership directory online, but they typically have the names and contact information for the decision makers of the business, since those people are the members of the Chamber. The other good thing about Chambers of Commerce is that they are typically comprised of small business owners and individuals. If you are focused on selling to this audience, local resources are often much better sources than national publications—small businesses are more closely tied to their area, so you will learn more about them and be more bonded to them if you read the same sources. It is definitely advantageous to learn what is happening in your community at large by reading local publications or checking local websites.

If you know what's happening in the local community, at the very least you will have several topics of conversation when you eventually get face-to-face with your prospect. Any kind of research will help you to better understand your prospects, since as an Accidental Salesperson, most of your prospects will be local, and be able to initiate an effective sales conversation.

I came across an old quote which holds true for anything to do with sales: "You are who you associate with." In other words, pick your relationships carefully; the sales community both for the Professional and Accidental Salesperson is built on trust and relationships. Whereas the right relationships and connections can help you to be successful in your sales efforts, the wrong relationships may ultimately hurt you. All the avenues of research I have talked about will help you learn more about your prospect. By knowing more about the person you are selling to, you will help position yourself as an expert in the field, and a reliable source of information. This is the first step towards building trust in a sales relationship.

The Accidental Salesperson Uses Information and Research

As an Accidental Salesperson, you don't need to use sales tricks in order to convince the prospect to buy. Remember that people buy from those they know, like, and trust.

Earlier in the chapter, we talked about research, and the benefits of planning and preparation. William is a perfect example of how the Accidental Salesperson can benefit from using research as a sales tool. He is a father whose son wants to play football. Being a protective parent, William worries about his undersized little boy playing such a physical sport, especially at the high school level. William's son has his heart set on playing on the freshman team, but that doesn't mean that William can't put in a sales pitch.

At the very least, William wants to make sure his son knows what he's getting into, so he starts doing research through the web and other outlets to prepare his sales pitch to his son. He gathers data on the high risk of injury, some permanent, from high school football. He finds an article from Sports Illustrated about the temptations and dangers of steroid abuse in high school sports. He has his son's tennis coach talk to him about other athletic options.

In the end, William will leave the final decision to his son, but as the Accidental Salesperson, he has successfully used information and research techniques to give himself a better chance at sales success.

Initiating the Sales Process

Whether you are a Professional or Accidental Salesperson, the approach to the first contact will be the same.

In its purest form, sales is about:

1) identifying a prospect
2) finding out what his needs are
3) showing him how your offer or proposal meets those needs

Regardless of how the salesperson makes contact with the prospect, each salesperson's approach should be the same, because every sales interaction centers around those three principles listed above.

At this point, you've learned about the importance of gathering information and research, and you're ready to interact with your first prospect. This may be a personal meeting, or simply a phone call. Phone conversations as a method of making the first contact are more challenging than face-to-face meetings since you will not have the benefit of being able to read the prospect's body language or get a clear reading of his emotions or feelings at each stage of the process. As we have discussed, the interpersonal relationship is key. For this reason, if you are making the first contact over the phone, make sure that you are short and to the point. It will be difficult to build a relationship in this format, so don't waste your time or the prospect's time. Let your prospect know why you are calling, and then you can begin the actual sales interaction.

You may find it helpful to have an agenda for phone calls in addition to having one for face to face meetings. This is just another reason why planning and preparation are important. All meetings should have an agenda, whether it is explicitly written or implied. Everyone's time is valuable, and a large benefit of having an agenda is that you can make sure that not only will no one's time be wasted, but you will be able to set the expectations for what will be covered during the meeting.

The Professional Salesperson uses an agenda that typically covers four action items:

1) **Introduce**—He'll introduce himself and explain why he was calling/meeting, giving a brief description of what he is selling/pitching or what he is looking for from the prospect.

2) **Ask**—He'll ask questions of the prospect in order to pre-qualify him, and find out what his needs are.

3) **Schedule**—If he is in front of a qualified prospect, the salesperson will set another appointment to continue the discussion.

4) **Wrap-up** (he'll thank the prospect for his time and then end the interaction)

Having an agenda ensures that the salesperson gets everything he wanted to out of the interaction. There will be no room for misunderstanding and he will be able to work more efficiently going forward.

Think about how this applies to your own life. For example, how many times have you had a simple conversation with someone when you later had a memory flash that made you say "I forgot … I should have asked her about _____;" or "I should have said _____?" It has happened to me plenty of times in both my professional and personal sales interactions and I'm sure it will happen again. Even though I prepare an agenda, there is always something that comes up. Sometimes, my excitement with the fact that I'm close to getting the sale gets in the way. However, having an agenda before any sales interaction is a simple step in planning to succeed. Like with most things in life, **preparation leads to success.**

When you, the Accidental Salesperson, approach a sales interaction, whether in person or on the phone, have an agenda and try to stick to it. Lay out the agenda along with the time expectations at the beginning of the meeting so that everyone is on the same page. Your prospects will respect you more because you are showing respect for their time.

The Professional Salesperson uses agenda-setting to create another way to pre-qualify his prospect. For example, if that salesperson sits down to meet with his prospect, then goes over his agenda and his prospect says to him "Wait. I didn't know that this was going to take an hour—I've got to get to another meeting in 30 minutes," the salesperson would then need to realign expectations. In this example, if the salesperson is able to cover everything in thirty minutes, then he will explain that to the prospect, and start his presentation. If he actually needs the whole hour, he might say something like "I'm sorry, but thirty minutes would not give me a chance to go over everything that needs to be covered. While we're sitting here in front of each other, can we take a look at your calendar to see when you would have a one-hour block of time available?"

Setting the agenda will even help the Accidental Salesperson get the upper-hand in a meeting. For example, pretend that you are a homemaker who is meeting with a painter to get a quote on painting rooms in the house. If you were to set the expectations at the beginning of the meeting by saying something like, "I only have thirty minutes to meet because I need to go to the grocery store," then you are ensuring that the painter will not waste your time and disrupt your plans by taking longer than a half-hour. Or, we can even apply agenda-setting to family dinnertime. Mom can set the agenda by saying, "We're going to be having dinner in ten minutes. Could you please wash your hands and set the table in time?" You can see how this serves to confirm expectations so that everyone involved knows exactly what's going to happen. It gives the kids a chance to raise objections like, "I don't want to stop playing yet. I'll be done in fifteen minutes."

The Importance of First Impressions in Your Sales Pitch

The Professional Salesperson is on the front lines of the business landscape. The company he works for is promoting a product or service and his job is to let people in the outside world know about it. This means that he has an incredible responsibility to the company—often times, he is a representative of what his company stands for, what the company offers, and how the company interacts with the rest of the business world. As an Accidental Salesperson, remember that you are a representative of whatever organization or business unit you are selling for, whether it is your law firm, your three-person business, your family, or yourself. The people you interact with will inevitably evaluate your sales offering in the context of their first impressions of you. Because of this, you should always make sure that you create a positive first impression with your prospects, whether on the phone or in person. Even the Professional Salesperson working for a large company that has been in the news, or is well known in the local area, can be responsible for either confirming people's perception of his company or changing it.

I remember times when I worked for AOL in the mid-1990s there were news-paper articles written about the company every day. Our competition even ran a commercial during the Super Bowl to advertise the perceived frustration of AOL users when they tried to dial-in and were faced with busy signals instead of a clear connection through the modem. On almost all of my sales appointments during that time, my prospects and customers would ask me about the state of the company. Of course, I didn't have the ear of the CEO or even know what was going on in upper management, but as a salesperson I was a representative of AOL, the company that employed me. I was trying to get people to place advertising on AOL. So, my prospects had valid concerns that if people were unable to get access to the service because of busy signals or whatever, then their ads would not be seen. Similarly, even when Microsoft launched MSN to compete with AOL, people wanted to know about the health of the company I worked for. After all, they were looking to advertise with a well-respected and stable organization.

My prospects were just going through the natural process of evaluation that would be conducted by any responsible businessperson—they were researching their options and would make a decision that would serve the best interests of their business. At the time, as an AOL salesperson, my prospects were looking to me to offer them reassurance, or even simply an honest evaluation of the company I was representing. During your sales efforts as an Accidental Salesperson, know that everyone you meet is looking for additional input regarding decisions that affect them or their company or business unit.

In most sales interactions, there is huge importance on the interpersonal rela-tionship. This all starts with the first impression. Think about the way that you first interact with your prospects. What do you believe is their first impression of you? If the first contact you have with a prospect is over the phone, how do you sound to them? Are you pushy and rude, or are you pleasant and compassionate? Are you able to make a good first impression over the phone? What about in a face-to-face meeting?

There are many more factors at work when you are meeting people in per-son for the first time. Face-to-face interaction is an important part of many sales exchanges.

There are two important factors of in-person communication which reach greater prominence when you initiate your first face-to-face sales meeting:

1) appearance
2) interpersonal skills

Appearance

You have probably heard the expression "dress for success." This is true, but when you are making a sales pitch, whether in a formalized business environment or outside of this, you not only need to dress for success, but you should dress appropriately for the particular prospect you are selling to. If you're going to the bank for a loan, you will dress nicer than if you were going to a family barbeque. During the course of pitching your product or service, you are also trying to get the prospect to be comfortable with you and respect you personally. This means that you need to look like you fit in, and not necessarily look like the best-dressed person in the room.

For example, let's look at the Professional Salesperson trying to sell gardening products to a family-owned landscaping shop. He is meeting with the head gardener, who spends his day working in the dirt and taking care of his plants. It would be pretty safe to assume that his prospect will probably be dressed in t-shirt and jeans, or similar work clothes. If the salesperson assumes this will actually be the case, would he show up in a three-piece suit, freshly shined shoes and a silk tie? This would probably impress Chairman of the Board at a multinational corporation, but in this case, his landscaping shop prospect will see him as an outsider, as just a salesperson. The salesperson would then have one strike against him as he starts to build the relationship with this particular prospect, working towards his goal of making the sale. This is not to say that in the example, the salesperson should show up to the meeting in a ripped t-shirt and jeans, but understand that he should make an effort to display a greater understanding of his prospect's business.

In the example above, by dressing appropriately, the Professional Salesperson is establishing an unspoken bond between him and his prospect by showing that he understands the business. At the same time, he is helping to put his prospect more at ease, while building the relationship, and building trust. Remember that people buy from those they know, like, and **trust**. Regardless of whether it is said aloud or not, if the prospect is wearing a t-shirt and jeans, and the salesperson shows up in an Armani suit, the prospect is uncomfortable. However, the Professional Salesperson can increase his chances of success by trying to figure out the dress code ahead of time. Planning leads to success and this kind of planning will help the salesperson make a good first impression.

Interpersonal Skills

At your first face-to-face meeting, part of your prospect's initial impression of you will be based on how you dress, simply because that's the first thing he sees. When your prospect first approaches you, he is building additional elements of his over-all perception of you. He may have spoken to you over the phone, but he now sees you in person and, and he will evaluate your face-to-face personality.

Remember that people buy from those they know and like, and trust. I can't stress this enough. Face-to-face interaction is the best way to build a relationship between two people. This is why politicians make stops at different cities across the United States instead of simply blasting TV commercials and radio ads every-where. Nothing can replace the bond you can establish by looking someone in the eye and shaking his hand. It is no different in sales, accidental or professional. Sure, many products are sold through an inside sales team that never sees their customer in person, but to truly achieve long-term success in sales, you need to learn how to make your face-to-face sales interactions an asset.

The interpersonal relationship is essential when making a sales pitch to any-one. The Professional Salesperson knows that it is important to do his back-ground research and know a little bit about the prospect with whom he is now face-to-face. There is no substitute for extensive planning and preparation. The Professional Salesperson does his research before building his initial prospect list, so he typically has a strong basic overview of the business or person he is meeting with.

One thing that differentiates a good salesperson from a great salesperson is his willingness and ability to go the extra mile by doing the necessary research. A great tactic used by the Professional Salesperson is that he will try to find out at least one piece of information about the prospect that is not readily available from common sources. If he is able to do this, he's got a great conversation starter which will accomplish two things:

1) sets him apart from his peers
2) shows that he cares about that prospect because he took the time to learn more about that business

Honestly caring about someone, whether it's a friend, an acquaintance, or a business prospect, will help to strengthen any relationship. Sales for both the Professional and Accidental Salesperson is a journey that starts when you first initiate the sales interaction, and really has no end. It's a journey, and along the journey, you should be working to develop a partnership both on a business level and a personal level. Early on in the process is the needs analysis phase, which I'll talk about later, where you are conducting an honest evaluation as to whether or not the result of your sales pitch can benefit your prospect. Throughout the entire sales process, your interpersonal communication should focus on building trust.

I just said that the "journey" of sales doesn't have an end. That's because your job as a salesperson does not end after you get the contract signed or you conclude the sales transaction in some other way. The Professional Salesperson knows that regardless of whether he is selling to a small business or an individual, the relationship never ends; even after he makes the sale. He will stay in touch with the new customer to make sure that the product or service he sold them is still living up to expectations, and also to ensure continued sales and referrals.

The Accidental Salesperson Makes the First Contact

Each of us has been a salesperson practically since birth. Even my five-year-old tried a sales pitch on me last week. She wanted to watch more TV before going to bed, so she tried to initiate a negotiation. Fortunately, I was strong in the objection-handling part of the sales interaction, and she went to bed on time. Maybe when she gets older, she'll read this book and be better prepared for the negotiation phase of the sales process!

Anyway, here's a good example of how planning and preparation can help an Accidental Salesperson at the first contact. Matt and Debra are both high-school seniors who have been dating a month, but Matt's got something looming in his near future—he's going to meet her parents for the first time. Matt, the Accidental Salesperson, needs to start gathering some sales skills together.

First impressions are key. Just like in the business scenario described earlier in this chapter, Matt, the salesperson, needs to gather information from different sources to make sure he can make the appropriate first impression. Just like a situation where the Professional Salesperson may have a point of contact inside the company, Matt has the perfect information source—Debra. So, he starts asking the basic information-gathering questions, just like the Professional Salesperson would. What does Debra's Dad like? What doesn't he like? What would impress him? How about Mom?

Matt gathers all of his information and prepares himself accordingly. When it was time for dinner with Debra's parents, he did a great job—he traded in his sweatshirt and ripped jeans for a nice pair of khakis and a starched shirt. He brought Debra's Mom a bouquet of daisies, which are her favorite. He was able to talk intelligently about topics that were interesting to Debra's father. As a result, the evening was a success. Matt did a great job of applying basic sales skills in an everyday sales situation.

Trackability and Accountability

It's one thing to plan out your sales activities by building an agenda or doing preliminary research about a prospect, but there are two other important elements of sales success—trackability and accountability. By *trackability*, I am referring to the way that successful salespeople track, or monitor in some way, their daily sales activities in an effort to discover a pattern which leads to successful sales. The successful Professional Salesperson will make sure to track all of his efforts. For example, if he makes cold calls to set-up appointments, he will track all of the outbound calls he makes. He may try to learn how many cold-calls it takes for him to get an appointment. Then he will learn how many appointments it takes for him to make a sale. This will help explain what his specific sales cycle is. **The "sales cycle" is how long it takes to make a sale from start to finish.** If he goes to net-working events in order to find new business, he will track things like which events give him the best prospects, or how many people he typically meets at specific events. What exactly is tracked will usually vary from salesperson to salesperson and from industry to industry. The Accidental Salesperson who is setting out to do something should try plan his activities and track the results in the same way.

Some good metrics professional salespeople track are: number of cold-calls or contacts, number of appointments, number of sales, average size of sale, average time to close. The goal of all of this, for any salesperson, is to standardize the sales effort, and hopefully even establish a dollar value to any component of the sales effort.

To use cold calling as an example, let's look at the Professional Salesperson focused on making outbound calls. He knows the following metrics:

- It takes him 10 outbound calls in order to set one qualified appointment
- He closes a deal on 20% of his appointments, meaning that he makes a sale every five appointments
- His average sale is $5,000
- He gets a 10% commission on every sale

Using these metrics, it takes him fifty calls to set the five appointments that will result in one sale, worth $5,000 on average. So, it takes him fifty calls to bring in $5,000. After further dissecting these numbers, he will see that every call is worth $100 in sales revenue ($5,000 divided by 50 calls). Factoring in his 10% sales commission, this means that every call is worth $10. *This is exactly why he makes those outbound calls.* If you were in his position, wouldn't you pick up the phone to call a prospect if you knew you'd be putting $10 in your pocket every time you did?

Tracking sales efforts leads to efficiency, which comes about by figuring out how to optimize the metrics that, in the end, will make the salesperson successful. The specific parts of the process can all be boiled down to these simple steps:

1) Learn the fundamentals
2) Implement the fundamentals and analyze the results
3) Adjust your new baseline of fundamentals

Let's look at each of these in turn:

Learn the fundamentals. The Professional Salesperson takes the time to figure out what is necessary for him to be successful in his industry, with whatever he is trying to sell. He won't just learn the basic skills of the trade, like being able to make hundreds of cold calls in a day or having strong follow-up skills, but he'll figure out the actual metrics for success. An example of a fundamental to learn within a sales job would be something like: "in order to sell this widget, I need to pick-up the phone 20 times a day." Maybe that metric means he will set up five appointments, which will get one sale. Or, "in my business, it is best to follow-up no sooner than one week after the initial presentation, but no later than two weeks." Or, for the Accidental Salesperson, it could be "in order for me to get my child to eat his vegetables, I need to cover it with chocolate." Regardless of what they are, these initial fundamentals are based on the history of sales success for whatever the salesperson is working on. In your accidental sales interactions, keep in mind that the fundamentals may change and evolve over time. For example, as your child gets older, his tastes will change, so the incentives to get him to eat his vegetables will most likely change. To that end, the next step, which is actually two steps in one, is to …

Implement the fundamentals and analyze the results. If you have followed the first step, you have figured out, historically, what it takes for you as a salesperson doing what you're doing, to be successful. Now it is time to implement the data you have into your daily sales behavior in the real world. Along the way, reconfirm as to whether or not those numbers are continuing to make you successful. Remember to **track the results**. Continuing the example of the Professional Salesperson from earlier, maybe he'll start out making 20 cold calls a day. Did twenty calls translate into one sale for him? Maybe after a month of work, he realized that he only needed to make 7 calls to make a sale. Maybe he needed to make 30. Maybe, using the Accidental Salesperson example from above, you can get your child to eat peas if they are mixed with applesauce, but not chicken, even though chicken works fine for your older child. The important thing is that you implement the fundamentals that work in each specific sales situation and then track the results, so you'll have a history of what it takes to be successful. Get as detailed as you can. You don't need to write everything down, just make sure that whatever you're doing, you track everything so that you can figure out what it takes to succeed. This brings us to the final step …

Adjust your new baseline of fundamentals. This brings you back to square one, where you have learned the fundamentals. Take a look at all of the information you have tracked. Were you as successful as you wanted to be? Make the adjustments which will help you maximize your time and efficiency.

That's all you need to remember when it comes to making yourself accountable. Learn, implement, analyze, and adjust.

I see two big benefits of a professional sales job. First, the Professional Salesperson's efforts are tangible. He can justify his performance through proof of his successful sales efforts. Think of all of the other office jobs that surround the Professional Salesperson. Most of them have no way to tangibly demonstrate their efforts. Sure, many companies now have goal setting and annual evaluations, but nothing beats the objective evaluation of looking at sales numbers. For example, if you are a general office worker, how can you clearly prove your worth to the company, other than taking care of the tasks that are assigned to you each day? A salesperson has a proven record of success.

The second positive aspect of a professional sales job is that it is a job that can be seen as a game. I love the competitive nature of sales. When I sell, I see every contract that I bring in as a small victory. Earlier, I talked about removing the stigma of being called a salesperson. Remember that **we're all salespeople.** Take advantage of the fact that whether you are a Professional Salesperson or an Accidental Salesperson, you can make that sales job fun. Being a parent is a common example of the Accidental Salesperson, and I can tell you that it is plenty of fun when I am dealing with my kids and I make a successful sale by getting them to come around to my way of thinking, or get them to behave for any small extended period of time. Of course, for the Professional Salesperson, it's not fun when he makes two hours of cold calls and gets hung-up on over and over again, but we're used to rejection.

As a salesperson, Professional or Accidental, you need thick skin because you will get rejected plenty of times. No salesperson is successful 100% of the time. Try to make sales a game and at the very least, you'll probably find that you will enjoy yourself more.

I just spoke of the competitive nature of sales. There is one characteristic inherent to every competition—the recognized metric of success. In golf, that metric is getting the ball into the hole in the fewest number of strokes. In soccer, it's scoring a goal to earn a point. If you are a bowler, your goal is to knock down as many pins as possible each time you roll the ball down the alley. In a political election, the goal is to get more votes than your peers. Sales is a competition. It is a competition for your prospect's acceptance, and a competition to earn benefits from your sales efforts. Since sales is a competition, it should have a recognizable metric of success. You are already tracking different elements of your sales activity, so set benchmarks for success. Then, reward yourself for hitting those metrics. Think about this if you were a parent—maybe your goal is to get your child to eat vegetables on four out of the seven days of the week—that's your metric for success. So, implement the fundamentals, whatever they might be, which would give you the best chance for success.

Throughout the process of tracking your efforts, decide on intervals where you will re-evaluate the benchmarks to see if they are accurate, but also remember that one of the keys to sales success is perseverance. Salespeople will get rejected, and they need to have the ability to push forward even when it is challenging. I honestly believe that if a determined person is selling a good product, the sales will come—it's just a matter of matching the needs of your prospect with the products or services that you are selling.

The Accidental Salesperson Utilizes Trackability and Accountability

Focusing on trackability and accountability is not only reserved for the salesperson monitoring his own efforts and making himself accountable. It is also a very effective sales management tool which will help yield better results in the long run for any activity. Kathy is a perfect example of someone utilizing these tools. She's an Accidental Salesperson as a volunteer who has been heading up a charitable foundation for several months, but now she is fully responsible for the fundraising benefit that the group will be hosting five months from now. There are many different things that need to get done, and she's going to be counting on many different people to help her reach her goal.

Kathy takes the first step towards conquering this huge task by listing out all of the things that need to get done in order for the fundraiser to be a success. She's utilizing the important sales skill of planning. The next step is to assemble the team that is going to help her. Once the members of her team start on the road toward completing their tasks, Kathy makes sure they are tracking their progress every step of the way. In the short-term, this ensures that each of her volunteers keeps on the pace and that all tasks get completed, but this tracking will also serve as a reference point in the future when she might be responsible for other events.

Once everything is completed, Kathy will know how long, for example, it takes to get a banquet table set for 50 people. Or, she'll learn that when ordering drinks, to make sure that the order gets placed at least two weeks before the event. All of that tracking will make her more efficient the next time around.

Whether you're a parent trying to get your kids to behave, a volunteer working at a fundraiser, or the CEO of an international company, the bottom line is that trackability and accountability in the short-run leads to efficiency and success in the long-run.

During the Sale

Before you initiate any sales interaction, remember the foundations of trackability and accountability for sales interactions that we talked about in the last chapter:

1) Learn the fundamentals

2) Implement the fundamentals and Analyze the results

3) Adjust your baseline

Everything that is included in the entire process of making the sale should focus on the end goal of the salesperson making a sales proposal which he feels would be a benefit to his prospect. As the Professional Salesperson develops his client base, he will remember to make sure that his product or sales solution fits his prospects' needs. The Professional Salesperson knows that his reputation precedes him, so he will make sure to be honest with his clients and prospects, and any other people that he interacts with in his sales universe.

> Sales is not about trickery, or deception. **Sales is about an open exchange of ideas which hopefully will result in a mutually beneficial outcome.**

In the world of the Professional Salesperson, most initial sales interactions are a *needs analysis.* In other words, a sit-down meeting where the salesperson is simply talking to the prospect, asking questions, and learning about his <u>needs</u>, goals, and concerns. At this point, the salesperson is trying to figure out if there is a potential for a successful partnership. He is literally conducting an analysis of the prospect's needs in order to confirm that the prospect is a good fit. This is by far the most important part of the sales process, but the Professional Salesperson will not try to sell anything at this time.

Regardless of what is being sold, the salesperson will never drop something in his prospect's lap and say "Do you want to buy this?" The goal of all sales interactions is a mutually beneficial outcome. The needs analysis is the first leg of the sales journey from point A to a point B, where Point B is the actual sale that results in mutual benefit for both the salesperson and the prospect. The best way for a salesperson to find out where that "Point B" is would be to conduct a needs analysis.

As I said earlier, during the initial interaction, the Professional Salesperson will typically not be selling the actual product or service he is pitching at that time. Instead, he will ask open-ended questions that will get the prospect thinking about solutions which could fit that prospect's needs. At the same time, he will help the prospect to feel more comfortable with potential options or opportunities that may be available. The end-goal of the sales interaction is to try come-up with a solution that works for everyone. Of course, this kind of solution might not exist with every interaction. This is why the Professional Salesperson will also use the needs analysis meeting to qualify the prospect. He will be trying to figure out if there is a potential sale as early in the process as possible.

Examples of the needs analysis interaction can be seen everywhere. I go through it on a daily basis with my kids. I have a son that will sometimes just start crying for no reason at all. Although sometimes I feel like yelling back at him to "just stop crying!" I quickly learned that it is more productive to apply some common sales techniques, most importantly, the needs analysis. So what do I do now when he starts to wail? I kneel down to his level and calmly ask:

"What do you need?"

"What do you want?"

"How can I help you?"

The response is typically something like, "I can't find my Matchbox car." (**Need:** Matchbox car) or "I spilled my drink." (**need:** clean-up and a new juice box). As most parents have learned when faced with similar situations, if the need is met, the problem is resolved. The same is true in sales of any kind—**if you meet the needs of your prospect, there is a good chance you will make the sale.** This fact is the reason for the needs analysis conversation.

In addition to learning about the prospect by engaging in open dialogue, the Professional Salesperson will make sure that by the end of this meeting he knows the answers to these three questions:

1) **Who is the final decision-maker?** He doesn't want to get into a position where the person he is selling to gives him the response, "I'm going to have to check with my boss/wife/husband." It doesn't matter how good a salesperson he is, he never wants a subordinate within any organization to deliver the final sales pitch.

2) **Is the decision-maker, or the organization, whether a company, or a family unit, in a position to accept his proposal?** For instance, do they have the money in their budget to buy? Are there any restrictions that would prohibit them from buying and using his product or service?

3) **What are the potential obstacles that stand between the salesperson and his ultimate goal of making the sale?** He will try to learn things like whether or not the decision-maker has any reservations about using his product, or whether the business unit has had a negative experience after they bought a similar service in the past.

No salesperson has a 100% success rate. I have lost out on many sales opportunities throughout my sales career, and in the end, some of those losses could be traced back to an issue that could have been resolved by asking the questions listed above. For example, I remember there were times when I was selling advertising that I was so excited to get in the door of a big company that I gave my best presentation to a Marketing Assistant. I would walk away from those presentations practically counting my commission check because I had given such a great pitch. I even left the meeting with the Marketing Assistant telling me "I love this proposal. Let me just get the OK from my boss and we'll get started." Needless to say, I never heard back from the ultimate decision-maker with approval on the proposal. Most of the time, I couldn't even get that Marketing Assistant to return my calls.

Throughout the process, the Professional Salesperson will try to qualify his prospects every step of the way, since his time is valuable and he always wants to make sure he is operating efficiently. The Needs Analysis is another step in the process. **Planning leads to efficiency, and efficiency leads to effectiveness.** He has already pre-qualified his potential clients from the beginning, when he created a prospect list based on the businesses he felt would benefit most from what he was selling. At the point in the sales process when he has the first needs analysis meeting, he needs to qualify again with the three questions mentioned earlier.

The first question in the Professional Salesperson's list of qualifiers I just talked about is extremely important. He always needs to find out who's going to be signing his checks. This could be different depending on each specific sales situation. In a small business, different employees are empowered to make many autonomous decisions. Even around my house, a small business unit of five, the different responsibilities have been delegated around the house. For example, my wife is completely in charge of the checkbook.

> The essential thing to remember is that when selling anything, it is important to not just find a decision maker, but you need to find your decision maker—you need to find the person who can make the decision on whether your sales pitch is accepted.

Going back to the example from when I was selling advertising, it is probably true that the same Marketing Assistant who couldn't pull the trigger on my advertising proposal was probably empowered to do many different things around the office without getting the official approval from her superior. Maybe she was empowered to buy all the supplies for trade shows. In other words, it was highly likely the assistant was actually the decisionmaker for some different issues around the office.

Regardless of what he is selling, the Professional Salesperson knows there will always be many different external factors that can affect his prospect. This is why he will constantly make sure that the prospect is still a potential sale or sales target. As he moves on to each successive stage in the sales process, the Professional Salesperson will make sure to qualify again and again. For example, even if he gets positive answers to those pre-qualifying questions at one point, he still needs to confirm that the initial information is accurate at every stage in the process. Time can change market conditions, the competitive landscape, pricing, etc. and thus change the factors that affect the prospect as well as the salesperson's own ability to make the sale.

The common mantra of most sales managers to their sales team is **A.B.C.** which means "Always Be Closing." For the Accidental Salesperson, in order to avoid mistakes and not waste time, he should *Always Be Qualifying*. Before you give your pitch, try to make sure to the best of your ability that the opportunity is right for you to make the sale. If you are constantly qualifying at every step of the way, you will not only ensure you are not wasting your time, but by getting confirmation on the current needs of your prospect, you will increase your chances of making the sale in the end.

In the Professional Salesperson's world, qualifying the prospect can be seen as a supplement to the earlier conversation about setting the agenda. Reviewing the agenda with the prospect is a great way to qualify him. The Professional Salesperson will let the prospect know what he hopes to cover in the meeting and possibly why he is going to go over those topics. If we assume that the salesperson's agenda is designed to be a process that needs to be followed in order for him to get the sale, then if the prospect does not accept that agenda, that person or business is probably not a good prospect.

Of course, needs analysis questions will differ, depending on the industry and the sales prospect.

> Here are typical needs analysis questions used by Professional Salespeople in common business-to-business sales environments:
>
> - What are some of your short term goals?
> - What are the metrics for success of this project? (In other words, the salesperson is asking how the implementation of his product or service will be judged.)
> - What challenges have you encountered in the past?
> - What challenges are you faced with now?

At first glance, these questions may seem a little slated toward the traditional business world, but we can look at how getting the answer to these questions can help the Accidental Salesperson by using the example owners of a clothing store I highlighted earlier. Let's pretend they are interacting with a customer who just came in the door. Here's how the needs analysis questions can be rephrased:

- What type of clothing are you looking for today? This is another way of asking about short-term goals.

- What types of clothes do you like best? Likewise, this is another way of asking, "How can my sales pitch be considered successful?"

- Are there any styles that don't particularly fit you well?

- Are you looking for an outfit for a specific event?

I encourage you to develop your own needs analysis questions, depending on what you are pitching and who you are pitching to.

During the needs analysis phase, one of the most important things a salesperson can do is listen to his client. It is during this phase that the proverb "silence is golden" comes into play. I'm sure you've come across people who love to talk. As a salesperson, it is tempting to jump in after every comment that the prospect makes and interject exactly how the product or service you're pitching can help answer the prospect's needs. However, in the long run, the salesperson will get greater benefit if he takes the time to listen to the prospect with as little interruption as possible. At this stage, the salesperson is just gathering information.

As you notice from the sample questions, all needs analysis questions should be *open-ended*. Open-ended questions give the prospect an opportunity to talk at great length about his needs. The more the prospect talks, the more information the salesperson will get; and throughout the sales process, **information is a key currency**. The more needs that you allow your prospect to express, the better your chances are of being able to meet those needs later on in the process. The more information you have, the more you will be able to show that you have a solution that fits the prospect's needs. This will also give you more ammunition for the negotiation phase, which may come later in the process. Not only will you increase your chances of making the sale, but you will save yourself the embarrassment of trying to sell something that your prospect doesn't need.

A proper needs analysis is crucial to sales success. I'll give you an example from my own life. Five years ago, my wife and I decided to get a dog. We brought the puppy home and decided that we needed to build a fence for our backyard, so that when she needed to go outside, we could just open the back door and let her do her thing without worrying that she'd wander off. We called on several different fencing places to give us estimates. I'll never forget one of the sales representatives that came out because the sales pitch he made sticks in my memory. That first rep came out and spent forty-five minutes going through his flip-book which high-lighted different fencing types, materials, information about why their fences last forever, customer testimonials, etc. At the end of the hour, our fence salesperson decided that we had a traditional house, so the best fence for us would be a picket fence that we could paint tan so that it would complement the trim on our house. There he was, selling us a product without any concern for our needs, or even knowledge of what the restrictions of our homeowner's association were. On top of that, a traditional picket fence has spaces between the wood slats, which did us no good, since our puppy would easily slip through the spaces in that kind of fence. Needless to say, he didn't conduct a thorough needs analysis, so he didn't know what we wanted, and he didn't get the sale.

The person who did get our business was basically a one man shop—he built the fence from scratch, and dug the holes by himself. Why did he get the sale? Mainly because he was observant—he didn't just come in and start pitching. Actually, the moment he came in, he started petting our dog and asked, "Is this why you need a fence?" That set off the whole conversation about our needs. Whether he did it intentionally or not, he was conducting a needs analysis. He asked open-ended questions that got us to talk about why we needed a fence, which was for the dog, but also to establish a measure of privacy, etc. In the end, probably because of the information he gathered, he was able to present a solution that fit our needs—a tasteful fence with no openings between the wood slats—a solution that is exactly what *we said* we wanted.

This brings up an interesting point about the needs analysis stage—this kind of interaction aims to get your prospect to tell you what he needs or he wants. An effective needs analysis actually makes the sales process very simple. **If your prospect tells you exactly what he needs and why, and you are able to deliver a solution that fits those expressed needs, then the odds are heavily in your favor that you will make the sale.**

Think about a needs analysis in the most basic terms—if you go out to a fast food restaurant and ask for a burger, they have a burger, so they sell it to you. Your server at McDonald's, the salesperson, just made a successful sale based on a 30-second needs analysis and the salesperson's ability to meet the prospect's needs. It may seem a little oversimplified in that example, but uncovering a prospect's true wants and needs is an aspect of the sales process that can be frequently overlooked, even by the best salespeople. But, if the salesperson can match the exact needs of his prospect, he'll make the sale most of the time.

The Balance of "Need" and "Value"

A person's buying decision is typically based either on his own personal evaluation of needs or of value. He will buy something because he needs it, or because the product or service being offered has some value to him. In today's economy, most products or services have a certain price associated with them, but **remember that the value of an item is what it is worth; price of an item is what it costs**.

The job of a salesperson is to increase the prospect's perceived need for whatever he is selling and/or increase the perceived value of what he is selling in the eyes of the prospect. A salesperson can increase the perceived need by identifying potential loss, and he can increase the perceived value by identifying potential gain. I will talk more in detail about these techniques, but the next two examples will give you an idea of the balance between need and value in making the sale.

Suppose that you're driving down the road and your tire goes flat. The fact is that you <u>need</u> a new tire. Within reason, you will pay the cost of replacing the tire, regardless of what it is because your car cannot drive without it. The nearest auto shop will then make the *sale* to you because you *need* a tire. They will make a sale based mainly on your urgent need, not necessarily on value. For the most part, in this example, price is not an issue. You may pay $80 for that tire at one shop, or you may pay $90 at another shop, but the bottom line is that you <u>will</u> buy the tire because your car is not able to run without it.

I can give another example using tires to explain how value comes into play. Let's go back to the example above and pretend that your tire did not just go flat. Maybe your tires are a little worn, and you're looking for a replacement. You don't have an urgent need yet; you're just looking around. There are many different options for tires—there's all-weather tires, tires that are better for performance cars, tires that are better in the snow, tires that last longer, etc. All of these options come at a different price. The exact tire you buy will depend on how well the tire matches the features that you perceive as having value. For example, it may be most important to you that the tires last for 80,000 miles. That particular tire may cost more than the all-weather tire that lasts for 50,000 miles. In this case, you will pay the higher price because the 80,000-mile tire is a better fit to the things you *value* in a tire.

Here's another example of how people can place value above cost. Several years ago, two local Dee Jays spent an afternoon driving around the Washington Area Beltway passing out money along the way. The DC Beltway is over 80 miles long, and there were people who spent their whole day following the "money van" around town for the chance to win a couple of dollars. So, the potential winners would drive all over the DC area, using up a tank of gas that cost about $20 for the chance to pick-up about $5. Would you ever pay $20 for a $5 bill? No one would. However, the fans of the radio show placed a *value* on being able to see the Dee Jays in person, so they were not factoring in the actual cost of their activity. Their main expense, which was the $20 tank of gas, was ignored because of the *value* they placed on seeing celebrities.

Sales that are based on need are often made after a more objective analysis. Sales based on value are often made because the customer has made some sort of emotional investment in the benefits of the product or service being offered. Remember that the purpose of a needs analysis interaction is to learn about a prospect's needs and values. The better a salesperson is at matching his product or service to the specific needs and/or values of his customer, the more likely he is to make the sale.

One important thing to note about needs analysis meetings is that when you are conducting a needs analysis, you should always be honest. Remember that sales are made based on trust and a strong relationship, even if that relationship is just in its early stages. Regardless of whether you are a Professional Salesperson pitching a business or an Accidental Salesperson pitching an individual or a small group, the purpose of a needs analysis meeting is for you to do an *honest* evaluation of whether or not whatever you are offering, or selling, is a good fit for that particular prospect. Trust and honesty go hand in hand. All salespeople should keep this in mind during the entire sales process, but especially at the needs analysis phase. Neither the Professional nor Accidental Salesperson should ever promote solutions that he doesn't believe in and should never pretend to know something that he doesn't.

To see a needs analysis meeting in action in a professional sales situation, here is an example of a technology salesperson selling a network server to a business:

PROSPECT: "Does your server come with XJL capabilities?"

The salesperson has no idea what this is, so he asks his prospect: "I'm not exactly sure about that—I've never been asked about XJL capabilities before. What do you typically use XJL for in your office?" *[**Note: This is a great way to spin the question, since the salesperson is essentially asking* *what this is needed for. Remember that the goal of the meeting is to uncover needs.]*

PROSPECT: "Well, we don't use that now, and I don't exactly know what it does. We just need to make sure that if our server goes down, we wouldn't lose all of our data. I was told that a server with XJL capabilities would take care of this for us."

SALESPERSON: "So, your main need is to make sure that the server you buy has a reliable data back-up system?"

PROSPECT: "Yes."

In this example, the salesperson was able to not only handle the situation, but also used the opportunity to get additional information about the needs of his prospect, like the fact that the company needed reliable data back-up. The benefit of this kind of open-ended discussion is that the salesperson may get the prospect to talk about needs that he didn't even know he had. In any sales interaction, the more information you have, the better off you will be.

If the Professional Salesperson gets to the end of a needs analysis meeting and he feels the prospect is still qualified, a great finishing statement that he may use might be:

"I'm going to work on a solution that fits your needs and bring it back to you. If you like it, what are the next steps?"

Regardless of whether you are in a professional sales environment, or you are an Accidental Salesperson, this kind of question is always useful in a sales interaction. It serves to confirm the prospect's decision-making timeframe along with the name of the decision maker. What the salesperson is trying to do at this stage is, again, confirm expectations and confirm information. There are many factors that swirl around the sales prospect or his business at any given time. Turnover rate may be high; people may get promoted into different responsibilities, the prospect may run out of money—anything may change. The challenge when selling is that each of these little tweaks could have a huge ripple effect on the overall business unit. This is why it is important for the salesperson to confirm the status of his sales pitch at every step of the way.

Another thing that the salesperson is doing by asking the question about next steps is that he may be getting his first sight of reaching his goal of making the sale. For example, pretend that we're looking in on the same salesperson at the end of his needs analysis call:

SALESPERSON: "I'm going to work on a solution that fits your needs and bring it back to you. If you like it, what are the next steps?"

PROSPECT: "If it fits our current needs, then we just have to go down to the accounting office to make sure that it fits in our budget."

[** *Note: At this time, the prospect has just thrown up huge signals for a follow-up question. By mentioning the accounting office, it means we're talking about money. They've practically written the final question for the salesperson*]

SALESPERSON: "How much are you looking to spend on the solution that fits the needs that you identified?"

PROSPECT: "We've budgeted $10,000 for this part of the business."

SALESPERSON: "OK. Thank you. I'll get back to work. While I'm here, though, can we pull out your calendar to see if you would be available at the same time next week so that I can present our solution to you?"

I intentionally inserted the part about setting the next appointment into the sample dialogue. In a professional sales situation, the salesperson will try to set the appointment during the current conversation. We're all busy, and we're all typically being pulled in hundreds of different directions at a time. By setting up the next appointment at the time of the current appointment, the Professional Salesperson can help his prospect commit while he has their attention. As a salesperson, there were many times where I left a prospect's office or talked to a prospect only to find that I was never even able to get them on the phone again. Once a salesperson gets on his prospect's calendar, it is harder, though, of course, not impossible, for that prospect to schedule something else in that time slot.

Going back to the sample conversation, by closing the meeting with "I'm going to go work on a solution…." The salesperson has allowed the prospect to lay out the path to sales success. He now knows that he will have a great chance of making the sale if he:

1) Shows how the product he is selling fits the prospect's needs

2) Keeps the budget under $10,000

Remember that throughout every sales process, it's important to confirm as many variables as possible along the way. If, in any sales interaction, you are able to boil things down to black and white issues, you've made a whole lot of progress toward making your sale.

The Golden Rule of Selling

Everyone is familiar with the Golden Rule, which is "Do unto others as you would have them do unto you." I want to introduce The Golden Rule of Selling:

> Sell unto others like you would have them sell unto you.

A large part of selling is relationship-building and creating long-term partnerships. Even if you are an Accidental Salesperson trying to get the best deal on a house painting job, for example, you should still aim to create a long-term partnership. You never know when you might want another part of your house painted. You wouldn't appreciate it if you went into a store and a salesperson just threw a product at your face and said "buy this." If that happened to you, chances are that you not only wouldn't buy whatever was being offered, but you may not visit that store again. Now tweak the situation a bit. Imagine that you walked into a car store and the salesperson sat down with you for five minutes and asked questions like:

"What kind of car are you looking for today?"

"Why are you looking at that kind of car?"

In other words, "What are your needs?" By performing a true needs analysis, the salesperson would be more likely to come up with a sales solution, in this case, a car, that best fits your needs. By listening to you, the prospect, he has just increased his chances of making a sale.

The Golden Rule of Selling should follow you through every step of the sales process—initial prospect interaction, whatever that might be—either with a business or your children, presentation/proposal, negotiating, etc. Always think about what type of sales interaction you would personally respond to, and this will give you clues as to how your prospect would want to be treated too.

Along those lines, try to make your early interaction with the prospect more relaxed. Sales cycles can vary considerably, depending on what you are selling, and who you are selling to. There's no need to rush anything. Take the time to learn about what your prospect needs and then try to determine where you can fit into his plans.

The Importance of Needs Analysis in the Sales Presentation

The needs analysis conversation will set the stage for success with the rest of the sales process. Remember that as the salesperson conducted the needs analysis, he was not only learning about the needs of his prospect, but he was also qualifying to make sure that his sales offering could help the prospect and that there was still the potential for a sale.

Of course, it is alright to find out that your sales offering can not benefit a prospect—you will actually earn more respect from the prospect if you are honest about the fact that there is not a good fit between the prospect's needs and the product or service you are offering. In such cases, you may even find that the prospect refers you to someone who may be a better fit.

Most importantly, after the needs analysis meeting or conversation, the salesperson can use the information he attains from this initial call in order to build a presentation that *answers his prospect's needs.* All salespeople win or lose sales based on how well they listened during the needs analysis phase and how well they can translate what they learned into an effective solution. Typically, people are resistant to change. Because of this fact, it is important for the salesperson to align his presentation so that it highlights how the sales offering is a solution that fits the prospect's needs.

When the Professional Salesperson starts to build his final presentation, he often finds it helpful to itemize his prospect's needs in front of him. He will find aspects of his product that are direct fits to his prospect's needs. If the prospect has specific needs that the salesperson cannot answer, he will think of alternative solutions which his product can deliver on. In other words, a salesperson can still be successful even if he only answers three out of their four needs, as long as he can show them that the lone outstanding need does not impede the prospect's overall goals or objectives. In this case, the Professional Salesperson will try to diminish the importance or priority of the need(s) that he cannot fill. Remember that the salesperson's main responsibility, based on the needs analysis meeting, was to bring back a solution that accomplishes the overall goal of meeting the needs of the prospect.

The Accidental Salesperson Conducts a Needs Analysis

Sometimes the information for a needs analysis doesn't have to be obtained solely from a face-to-face meeting. Tom is a painter who is always looking for more work. Like any good small business owner, he can never have too many jobs. A responsible businessman knows that one of the keys to success is having options. The more options you have, the more chances you have to make the right choice—the choice that leads to success.

Tom would never call himself a salesperson. He would be more than happy just painting houses and collecting a paycheck on each job. However, this one particular day Tom, the Accidental Salesperson, conducts a needs analysis just by using common sense. He was walking by one house on his way to lunch and saw that there was a construction worker out on the front lawn sawing different pieces of wood which would be used for the renovation of that home.

Most of a needs analysis should be done through direct communication with the prospect, but some things can be inferred. By seeing the construction work at the house, it was pretty safe to assume that those raw materials would be put up in different parts of the house. After those raw pieces of wood were put in the right place, chances are they would need to be painted. However, this was all just an educated guess. He would need to find out more information.

The next day, Tom rang the doorbell at the same house and talked to the homeowner to conduct the same type of needs analysis that a Professional Salesperson would. After he introduced himself and explained a little bit about his services, he asked questions like:

- "I noticed you had a contractor sawing some wood out in your front yard. Are you doing some renovations?" It's important to ask the obvious question because the obvious question established some common ground which the prospect can then expand on.
- "What are you having done?"
- "Will you need anything painted?"
- "When will those renovations be completed?"

By taking the time to ask these questions, Tom is not only getting himself closer to one particular sale, but he will also get on the road to expanding his customer base.

The Heart of the Sales Interaction:
The Presentation

The Importance of Confidence in a Sales Presentation

Regardless of how sophisticated your sales pitch is, at this point in the process, let's assume you have already prepared a sales pitch that completely answers your prospect's needs, and you are ready to deliver your proposal. Before the first words of that pitch come out, keep in mind that one of the most important components of an effective presentation is <u>confidence</u>—you need to believe that what you are pitching can have a benefit to both you and your prospect, and that you are honestly working toward a win/win resolution.

Whether you are consciously aware of it or not, your confidence, as it is projected to your prospect, has a direct affect on his perception of whatever you are pitching. As a result, this has an effect on your likelihood to make the sale.

If you are a parent, think about the importance of confidence. In which situation will your children respect your authority more:

1) You timidly ask them to go to bed on time.
2) You confidently send them to their rooms after highlighting the disciplinary consequences of not agreeing to your *sales pitch*.

When I was a sales manager at AOL, whenever any of my salespeople where in a slump, I tried to remind them that prospects can smell fear and intimidation on a salesperson. Lack of confidence can kill a sales presentation and send a salesperson deeper into a slump. However, the opposite is almost always true—if a confident salesperson is pitching a good product or service, then he will eventually make the sale.

Again, here's an example from my own life. I had been a successful salesperson at AOL for eight years. I was usually on top of the national sales rankings as an individual, and when I was promoted to manager, I shaped my team into one of the strongest sales groups in the country. Then, I left for an opportunity with a small start-up company. I was brought in as the only sales rep, and I had the responsibility of figuring out how to make the service marketable. In other words, the service I was selling had not previously been sold to businesses outside of contacts related to the company's founder. My job was to figure out the formula that would allow the service to be sold to a wide range of businesses by using a strictly proactive sales effort.

I had come from eight years of media sales at AOL, and before that, I worked at a local radio station and then also with an advertising agency. Again, these were all media sales jobs. The new start-up I went to work for after AOL focused on selling information technology services, which is something I had no experience with. Actually, my lack of experience was one of the black marks against me when I interviewed for the position. In the end, I think that I got the job because I kept telling the Owner and the Board of Directors that the fact that I didn't have any experience with technology sales was irrelevant. I told them the same thing I've been telling you in this book—**all sales interactions are based around the same foundations**. All I needed to explain was that I had a proven track record as a successful salesperson by using the *needs analysis* approach to sales.

> Anyone can be a salesperson if they follow the basic sales principles.

When I was on those interviews, I knew that whether I was selling advertising to a car dealership, selling clothes in a retail store, selling fences to homeowners, or selling technology services to small businesses, the basics of sales remained the same—learn the needs of your prospect and then deliver a solution that meets those needs.

Now back to the importance of confidence—needless to say, I was a little out of my element when I first got started at this new job. Even though I studied every day in an effort to understand the technical terms and learn more about the industry, there was still some hesitation in my sales pitch. My wife told me that I was lacking confidence, and that was affecting sales, but I didn't believe her. I was sure that, even though I wasn't completely comfortable with the technological terms, I was still projecting knowledge and confidence to my prospects on the outside world. After all, I believed in the product, and I thought it would be a good fit for my prospects' needs. So, I drifted along in one of the worst sales slumps of my career, thinking that I was projecting confidence on presentations, but failing to make the sale. Then, for whatever reason, I got my first signed contract. That was all it took to get the ball rolling. Did I change my pitch? No. Did I dress differently? No. As the sales started coming in, I realized that *confidence* was the deciding factor. Even though I was trying my hardest to make the sale, I realized that I did not honestly believe I could be a successful salesperson for technology services. All I needed was to break through with the first sale, and the one block to my confidence was cleared. The sales quickly followed.

Even if you are an Accidental Salesperson, I'm sure you wouldn't be evangelizing something that you didn't believe in. So, let people know it—project confidence and you will increase your chances of making the sale. If you are worried that your sales efforts may be cursed by lack of confidence, ask for another opinion. A third-person point of view could always be useful. If you honestly believe that your sales offering can benefit your prospect, those prospects will believe it too, and you'll make the sale.

The Sales Presentation

After all the planning and preparation, information gathering, and needs analysis, you are now ready to make the sales pitch to your prospect. You've filled the proposal with examples of how your offering is a great match to the prospect's needs, how your product fits into all the parameters that he laid out, and how both parties, the salesperson and the prospect, will be benefiting from the transaction. You're done, right? If you are a Professional Salesperson, you can start counting your commission because it's in the bag. Not so fast.

Of course, as salespeople, we will always have the threat of objections hanging over each sales pitch, regardless of whether it's a 30-second phone pitch, a five-minute negotiation with our children, or a complete face-to-face presentation. I'm going to talk more about handling objections in the next chapter, but at this point, I want to talk about one of the more important elements of a sales presentation—*anticipating objections* before they hit.

In this case, as with most things, planning and preparation lead to success. The first step in any sales pitch is to confirm with your prospect that nothing has changed since your last meeting and that there is no discrepancy between the information you had gathered and the present reality. Often times you will find that objections arise because there is some kind of disconnect between the salesperson and the prospect. It could be over expectations, money, price, or many other things. Maybe, for example, the problem that you were going to solve for them has resolved itself and they no longer have a need for whatever you're offering.

Remember what I was saying about having an agenda? You can help to confirm understanding between you and your prospect at this stage in the process by setting the agenda at the beginning of the meeting. This agenda should serve the same purpose as the agenda you laid out when you made the first contact with the prospect. It doesn't need to be fully written out and documented. All you need to do is let your prospect know exactly what will happen during the meeting or conversation, along with your expectations of this specific interaction. In polite language, let the prospect know from the beginning that you will not waste their time, and you don't expect them to waste yours. The best way to do this is to reference the information that you learned during your needs analysis meeting. Highlight some of the things they previously told you, or things you had learned from your research. You want the prospect to see that you have listened to their needs, worked to build a proposal based on the information that you have gathered, and that you now need to confirm facts to make sure nothing has changed in the interim. For example, one opening to a meeting that a Professional Salesperson might use is:

"Thank you for taking the time to meet with me again. I have put together a business proposal based on the notes I took during our last meeting. Before I begin, I just wanted to confirm some of the issues we talked about." [*Note: At this time, he would review everything he uncovered at the last meeting, during the needs analysis phase, along with the decision-making criteria for accepting the proposal, budget, etc.*]

As an Accidental Salesperson, just remember the Golden Rule of Selling, and remember that your goal as a salesperson is to deliver a solution, through a product or service, that helps answer a need that your prospect has. To that end, you will find that everything keeps coming back to the needs analysis meeting or information-gathering phase. This part of the sales process serves to build the foundation for all future interactions with the prospect.

The purpose of all your preliminary research and the needs analysis meeting is to learn about the needs of your prospect. However, at the same time, you are also trying to uncover some of their concerns and fears. This is why it is so important to conduct a thorough needs analysis. If done properly, you'll increase your chances of making the sale in the end.

Always remember to keep strengthening the relationship by building trust throughout the sales process. During that first meeting the Professional Salesperson had, he was not approaching the prospect as a salesperson—he was simply a fellow businessman having an open discussion with his peer. In this case, since he was not initiating the discussion in sales mode, the prospect's defenses might be down, and he will be more likely to give the salesperson a complete and honest picture of his situation. For example, if the Professional Salesperson hears that his prospect was burned by a different salesperson a year ago, he'll take note of this. If the salesperson is unable to come up with a sales presentation that shows he is a trustworthy partner, he will likely face that same objection later in the sales process.

> Listening is one of the most important skills that any salesperson, Professional or Accidental can have.

As your prospect lays out his issues, needs, and concerns throughout all stages of the sales process, you will start to be able to see the road map for your future sales success.

As I have outlined, the two factors that need to be taken into consideration for any sales pitch are *need and value*. I've talked about the process of a needs analysis where you are evaluating a prospect's needs and figuring out potential objections, but then you can also use the information you gather to determine which things are valued by your prospect. Again, the more information you can get, the better off you will be.

In general, people buy because they have an unyielding **need** for a product or service, or because they have a high perceived **value** of the product or service. Regardless of who you are pitching to, your sales presentations should show how whatever you are selling meets one of those criteria.

Increasing Need by Identifying Potential Loss

Throughout the sales process, and especially in the needs analysis phase, the salesperson is focused on identifying the specific needs of his prospect and also determining what things are valued. The salesperson will always help his chances of making a sale if, during the sales presentation, he stays focused on increasing the perceived need that the prospect has for the sales offering or increasing the perceived value of it.

A great way for a salesperson to increase the perceived need of a product is to *identify potential loss*. In other words, the salesperson will highlight what the prospect would be missing if he didn't accept the product or service being pitched. For example, let's look at the professional digital camera salesman, trying to sell his cameras to a local marketing firm. He has already gone through the initial stages of pre-qualifying the business so he's learned that they manage events all over town and they need to take pictures at these events so they could then run those photos as publicity shots. The firm is not completely sold on his product, the digital camera, because they currently feel comfortable in using the traditional cameras that they have always used. As stated earlier, the salesperson will get closer to making the sale if he can increase his prospect's perceived need for his product by identifying potential loss.

One consistent metric that a Professional Salesperson often uses to show potential loss is that he highlights a potential loss of *profit* to that business or individual. The potential loss of money will definitely get the attention of any prospect. As we've discussed, money affects everything. Specifically, allocation of money. All business units try to keep their spending within a pre-defined budget. Even individuals, and the "business unit" of the family will often make decisions whether or not to buy things based on how much money they have. On a daily basis, most people are in a personal battle to try to make each dollar go farther because they are traditionally stretched thinner than they would like to be. In this example with the Professional Salesperson, it would help the salesperson's chances of making the sale if he is able to show how his prospect's loss of profit could be a direct result of not buying his product.

Another way to show loss is by demonstrating a potential loss of *opportunity*. Using this tactic, the salesperson highlights that his prospect may lose market share to the competition, or they might let other businesses gain a competitive advantage because of any delay, or failure to implement what he is selling. Time is a strong ally if the salesperson is trying to identify potential loss.

Here's how a sample conversation utilizing the sales techniques I just talked about could go:

PROSPECT: "I'm not sure if we're going to buy your digital cameras. We're pretty happy with the traditional cameras we've used in the past."

SALESPERSON: "I understand your hesitation. It's a big step to change the products that you have traditionally used [**Note: *The salesperson is showing empathy for his prospect—another step in building a strong relationship*], but there are several advantages to using a digital camera. Let me ask you something—in the past, how many rolls of film did you go through at your last event?"

PROSPECT: "Probably around ten rolls."

SALESPERSON: "Why did you use up so many rolls?"

PROSPECT: "Well, we take a lot of pictures because typically, of the two-hundred and fifty pictures we take, we only end up with about twenty-five really good ones."

SALESPERSON: "How much does it cost you to develop the pictures?" [**Note: *The salesperson is going down a path that will ensure understanding. He's putting it in monetary terms, which everyone can understand*]

PROSPECT: "Probably about $7 per roll, so we spend about $70 per event."

SALESPERSON: "$70 for 25 pictures that you can keep. That's almost $3 a picture. Did you know that if you use a digital camera, you could actually see each picture you take immediately after you take it? This way, you can make sure you have a good shot. Then, you only need to develop the pictures that you want. If you had a digital camera for the last event you worked, considering that most photo developing places only charge about 20 cents per print, you would have only paid a total of about $5 for those 25 good pictures. [**Note: *At this point, the salesperson has just identified one potential loss—the loss of profit. The salesperson has just told his prospect that the digital camera would have saved the company $65 just at their last event alone. To put this another way, the salesperson has helped* *the prospect see that if they don't buy a digital camera, then they will essentially be wasting $65 for every event that they cover from here on out—a costly potential loss of money. [Of course, in today's world, most professional PR shops see using digital cameras as a no-brainer, but I'm trying to build a simple example.]*

PROSPECT: "That's a good point, but I'm comfortable with the camera I've always used."

[***Note: This is a common response from prospects, remember, as we've discussed, most people are much more comfortable with the status quo, but nevertheless, the prospect is still not convinced. Now is the time for the Professional Salesperson to try to focus on another way where he can identify potential loss …]*

SALESPERSON: "Another great thing about our digital cameras is that when you take a picture with a digital camera, you know that each shot is being recorded. After you take the picture, you can see on this digital display that the picture was actually taken. Have you ever had a roll of film not develop because your photographer may have put the film in wrong or because the roll was accidentally overexposed?"

PROSPECT: "You're right. We always have to count on losing one or two rolls."

SALESPERSON: "With your traditional camera, you could take great pictures, only to find out that you'll never see those pictures because the film was put in wrong. With a digital camera, you won't have to worry about missing a key moment at an event." [***Note: The salesperson has now just identified another potential loss—the loss of opportunity. In other words, an event only happens once. After that event has passed, the prospect can't take another picture.]*

Increasing Value by Identifying Gain

I have just finished talking about increasing need by identifying potential loss. Of course, the word "loss" has a negative connotation, just as the word *need* implies being in a desperate situation. If you feel uncomfortable trying to make a sale by identifying negative factors in your sales pitches, another way to get yourself closer to a sale is by focusing on the more positive benefits that your product or service could deliver to your prospect. When you talk about *value*, you are typically working within a positive association.

Value can be *tangible*, as in a direct analysis of future savings, meaning that one is able to see a definitive financial gain, or it can be assumed. By *assumed value*, I am referring to value that someone places on an object or a service that is not able to be measured monetarily.

> Assumed value is subjective, whereas tangible value can be analyzed objectively.

The only difference between increasing your chances of making the sale by identifying potential loss or potential gain is in the delivery of your presentation. For instance, in the last example, the salesperson was angling the conversation to show how sticking with a traditional camera would result in a loss to the business of $65 per event. He could have just as easily talked about the fact that using a digital camera could save the company $65 per event. This is an example of tangible value—a direct analysis of future savings, since people value their money.

Similarly, along the lines of the discussion regarding the negative consequences of the photographer putting the film in wrong, the salesperson could have talked about the emotional effects, peace of mind, of making sure the precious pictures won't be lost after an event that only happens once. This would be an example of assumed value.

The decision as to which approach to use will also depend on your prospect. When you are pitching to different people, you will run across a wide array of personality types, both across different offices and within the same community. Some people focus more on the bottom line, and can only really accept presentations when comparing historical data. This type of personality would require a sales approach that is focused on need or on a value proposition that is more tangible. These are the types of people who are resistant to change because the status quo is known. In this situation, you would focus on identifying potential loss if things stay as they are in order to increase your prospect's perceived need, and try to get them to take definitive action. On the other hand, you may find during your needs analysis that your prospect is looking to use your product or service to make a mark within his company, or to get a similar type of positive recognition. In this case, you should focus on the <u>value</u> that you could bring to his office since *value* is innately subjective. In the end, regardless of who you are pitching to, the more information you have on a prospect, the more prepared you will be to develop a sales approach which will give you the best chance for success.

More Examples of the Need for Understanding

Throughout the entire sales process, the Professional Salesperson will also be focused on gaining understanding to make sure that he and the prospect are on the same page. During the needs analysis stage, as the salesperson was learning about his prospect's needs, he continually asked for understanding at each step. He confirmed the prospect's specific needs to make sure nothing was overlooked. When the salesperson started the sales presentation, he reviewed his notes from the last meeting to make sure that the needs hadn't changed, or also to make sure that other variables hadn't changed.

The Accidental Salesperson should always be trying to gain an understanding of the situation along the way. It's not just a case of the more you know, the better off you are, it's the more you <u>understand</u> that will help you in the end. This is why, throughout the sales process, it is important to speak in common language to your prospect. In other words, don't give a pitch using language that your prospect can't understand. This is especially true for the parent who has been put in the role of Accidental Salesperson—make sure your kids understand what you're saying to them, or your "sales interaction" will go nowhere. Again, this is so that you both can stay on the same page as the presentation progresses. Psychologically, mutual understanding in any interaction will typically strengthen the bond between the two parties and pave the road to your sales success.

The Accidental Salesperson or Professional Salesperson, throughout the actual sales presentation, should make sure there is understanding along the way. When you list a specific need that your product or service answers, make sure that your prospect understands exactly how it meets his needs. Of course, you don't need to be patronizing to him, just do whatever makes you feel comfortable so that you know he understands how whatever you are selling meets his needs. In other words, you don't need to stop each step of the way and ask if he understands, but you can get creative.

Here's a quick sample dialogue. I'll use the example of the digital camera salesperson I talked about earlier. Let's say that the prospect had an expressed need to not waste money on film:

SALESPERSON: "By using a digital camera, you only develop the shots that you want. This way, you won't ever be faced with a situation where you pay to have a whole roll of film to be developed, only to find out that four out of the twenty-four pictures on the roll were actually usable. Of course, digital cameras don't need film. Would you be OK with the fact that you would never need to buy a roll of film again?"

[**Note: this is an open-ended question that tests for understanding without directly asking it. The salesperson is making sure that the prospect understands the way that digital cameras work—in other words, the business would not need to buy film.]

PROSPECT: "Of course we'd be fine with that. We spend so much money on film every month. However, how is the picture quality as compared to a traditional camera?"

[**Note: Here is the first objection—when this happens, the salesperson will try to not get into a back-and-forth match with his prospect over each objection. If possible, he will save all objection-handling until the end.]

SALESPERSON: "Actually, it's hard to tell the difference. I know that was one of your concerns the last time we met, so I brought some information about that which I'll go over a little later."

[**Note: The salesperson is not allowing the prospect to control the meeting. Remember the agenda that was set at the beginning of the meeting should have been that he was there to show the prospect how the solution fits his needs. The salesperson will stick to the agenda, so he can make sure he covers everything he needs to. At this stage, the focus is on making sure that the prospect understands each element of what is being offered, not answering objections.]

Regardless of how the exact conversation goes, the salesperson needs to make sure that both parties are on the same page. Lack of understanding leads to objections. Objections get in the way of making the sale.

Additional Tips for Presenting

One tip for your sales presentation is to try to simplify your product or service. Try to explain what you are selling in terms that your prospect can understand. This means you should use common language, since slang or industry jargon may be confusing to your prospect. No matter how good your pitch is, people will not buy things they don't understand. For technology salespeople, it might be especially challenging, since the value they bring to businesses would typically be a product or service which features new terminology based on the new technology. If his product is extremely complicated, the Professional Salesperson usually finds it useful to have leave-behinds, or graphical examples that might help explain things better, or maybe even material that he could later mail to his prospect.

With most prospects that salespeople face, small changes can have a big impact. As you are presenting, whether in a formal presentation if you are the Professional Salesperson or a casual conversation as the Accidental Salesperson, make sure to keep this in mind because it is definitely running through the mind of your prospect. These are the things that prospects worry about. Whether it's rational or not, every concern your prospect has needs to be considered as a valid concern.

The Professional Salesperson knows that the ideal pitch should show that the product or service he is pitching will have minimal disruption to the daily lives of that prospect, but have a huge positive impact in either short-term or long-term. Whether he is selling office supplies, mail delivery services, IT infrastructure, whatever; the Professional Salesperson will show how the implementation of what he is selling will not negatively impact the prospect's life. He'll focus on showing the prospect a turnkey solution, which means that it will integrate seamlessly into the current environment, since it will be an uphill battle if the product or service appears to disrupt the prospect's environment too much.

Regardless of what you are selling, the status quo is one of your most imposing enemies. Therefore, after you have laid out the basic information regarding your sales pitch, you then need to take the next step to explain the implementation process as it relates to your sales offering. Highlight both short-term and long-term effects. Sometimes, like in the fundraising example from earlier, the implementation process is minimal. In that case it's just accepting a donation. However, in more complex scenarios, you should help to guide your prospect with respect to his expectations and the expectations that you established at the beginning of the sales process. This will deliver an extra level of comfort to your prospect, since you will be helping him to envision just how good your product or service can be.

Let's use a new product to highlight one example of what a salesperson could say in order to relay this point to his prospect. In this case, the Professional Salesperson is selling a machine that helps offices run more efficiently. This is a product which prints valid postage stamps on letters and packages. We're calling it the *Mail Wizard 1000*. He's quickly able to explain implementation and review its benefits.

> SALESPERSON: "So, as you can see, by using the Mail Wizard 1000, you will save time in the short run, since you won't have to manually process incoming and outgoing mail, and also the time you save will help your business run more efficiently going forward. For example, your assistants can use the extra time to do additional work that they might not have been able to get done before."

Of course, this is just an example, but the key parts of that quote were that the salesperson gave the prospect an example of an immediate benefit that his product delivered. He then followed that up by helping the prospect to paint a mental picture of benefits that would be realized in the future.

Any salesperson in this position should look to go back to his notes from the needs analysis stage for information, since it would be even more advantageous if the example he gives in his presentation relates to one of the specific needs that were previously identified by the prospect. Remember that one of the keys of sales is matching the prospect's needs with your product or service. Keep this in mind, and remember to qualify the prospect at every step of the way, and you'll be in good shape.

The Accidental Salesperson Gives a Presentation

As we've talked about, sales are simply a part of everyday life. Chances are you've been a salesperson pretty much since the time you could talk. Dan is another example of an Accidental Salesperson. He's a 17-year-old high school senior who is trying to get his parents to lend him the car so he can go out with friends.

This is going to require a pretty tight pitch in order for him to make the sale. In this case, *making the sale* means getting permission to have the car for the night. Before Dan talks to his parents, he goes through a mental checklist of the components of a successful sales presentation:

- He'll make sure he knows about his prospects, who are his parents.
- He'll figure out their needs.
- He'll then give a sales pitch that shows how the thing that he is selling still meets the needs of his prospect.

In this scenario, Dan can't really do a full sit-down needs analysis meeting. However, he's lived with his parents for over 17 years, and this topic of borrowing the car has come up several times in the past, so Dan is confident that he has a good understanding of his prospects, as well as their specific needs. He knows what their objections will be ahead of time so he will make sure that all elements of his sales presentation will not only show how he will meet their needs, but he will focus his presentation to answer objections before they come up.

Then, Dan starts off on his presentation. He tells his parents that he understands they would be concerned with him taking the car because who knows where he'd be driving, and what he'd be doing with the car. What if he was taking the car to do some street racing? What if he's going to be driving a long distance away from home? Is he a good enough driver? What if he tries to pack eight kids into a five-person car to go joy-riding?

So far, so good. Dan is doing a great job of showing the prospects that he understands their need for peace of mind.

Dan continues through his presentation in this manner, so he is answering the objections before they officially come up. If there is a chance his parents might be concerned about his itinerary, he's going to answer that ahead of time:

"Mom and Dad, I'm just going over to Sean's house to watch some of the football game on TV with Pete and Will. Then, we're going to go to the movies."

Then, Dan outlines additional benefits:

"I know my curfew is 11:00. Since I'll have the car, I'll be completely in control of my own schedule, and I will definitely be home in time for curfew. If I had to rely on one of my friends for a ride, I'd be counting on them to drop me off as well, and I might be late. Or, you would need to come pick me up."

Lastly, in order to seal the deal, Dan, the Accidental Salesperson, goes above and beyond. Here's the closer:

"I noticed that you have less than a half-tank of gas in the car. I'll make sure to fill it up for you."

In the end, Dan made the sale. As with any sales situation, you can increase your chances of making the sale by making sure your sales presentation shows how you can meet the needs of your prospect.

The Salesperson's Worst Fear: Objections

I am not a fan of all the various "closes" that different sales gurus promote. The Professional Salesperson who has been in sales long enough probably knows all of them all by heart: the "Ben Franklin" close, the "My Dear Old Mother" close, the "Puppy Dog" close. I'm not going to waste time going over each of these. Just check your local sales book for details on these and thousands of other closes.

In my view, a prospect should never be *closed*. A salesperson doesn't need to trick the prospect into accepting his pitch by using a slick sales tactic. In any kind of sales, whether you are a Professional Salesperson selling to a small business or to a large firm, or an Accidental Salesperson selling to your parents, as in the last example, **the focus of the sales interaction should be on coming to a mutually beneficial agreement.** If you have done a complete needs analysis, and if you have pre-qualified your prospect along the way, whoever that might be, then the act of your prospect signing off on your service contract, or accepting whatever you are selling, is simply the next logical step in the process. This is not to say that there aren't a myriad of factors that could derail this process. As we have discussed before, every prospect can be deeply affected by small changes in his environment, personal changes, etc. All of these factors can affect the potential success of the salesperson, Accidental or Professional, by allowing new objections to surface.

Any salesperson should simply see objections as requests for more information. If a prospect is asking a question, or presenting a challenge to what the salesperson is selling, it actually is a sign that he is interested. Think about it—if the prospect wasn't interested, why would he ask a question? After all, it takes some thought to come up with a question to ask. The prospect could have just as easily ignored the salesperson. If the prospect formulated a question, then he was thinking about what the salesperson was pitching. If he was thinking about what the salesperson was pitching, he is at least a little bit interested in eventually *buying* what the salesperson is selling.

When a prospect poses a question or makes an objection, the salesperson's first task should be to help the prospect identify *tangible* objections so each objection can be dealt with in context. Another reason to make sure that every objection is tangible is so that, as a salesperson, you don't waste your time trying to kill ghosts. By this, I mean that you should make sure that the prospect can explain his objection in detail, and in concrete terms. For example, if your prospect simply says, "I don't like it," that's not a tangible objection. Look at this sample dialogue for clarification. We'll go back to the example of the Professional Salesperson selling the Mail Wizard 1000:

SALESPERSON: "Now that you've seen everything my product has to offer, do you agree it could benefit your office?"

PROSPECT WITH AN OBJECTION: "I don't know. It just doesn't seem right."

SALESPERSON: "What part of our product doesn't seem right? Is there a specific concern that you have about the Mail Wizard 1000?"

[**Note: This is a great move by the salesperson to help his prospect create a tangible objection. If the salesperson is looking to get a specific answer, he might as well ask the prospect directly for a specific answer)

PROSPECT: "Actually, I don't understand how the Mail Wizard knows how to put on the right postage. And, how do I know that when it puts on the postage, that the Post Office will recognize it as a valid stamp?"

SALESPERSON: "I can explain that to you. However, other than these two concerns, do you like everything else about what I'm offering to you?" [**Note: The salesperson is not answering each objection in turn, he's getting everything out on the table]

PROSPECT: "Yes. It really seems to be a good product; it's just that my main concern is that the Post Office won't recognize a stamp from the Mail Wizard as legal postage."

There are now two tangible objections:

1) How is the right postage put on?

2) Will the post office recognize it?

and the prospect has even indirectly ranked them in terms of importance, so the salesperson can start answering those specific objections.

There are a couple of things to notice from that dialogue. The first is that the salesperson worked to turn the prospect's vague objection into a concrete concern. If the salesperson would have left things at "It doesn't seem right," he would probably still be answering the objection today. Remember the need for understanding throughout a sales presentation. The salesperson, Accidental or Professional, has focused on understanding at every step of the process, so he shouldn't let up just because he is getting closer to the end of the process. During any sales interaction in your daily life, if you get objections, make sure that both you and the prospect have an understanding as to what the tangible concerns are.

The second thing to notice from the dialogue is that after the prospect gave a specific answer to his first objection, the salesperson asked for more. It is always helpful to get all objections out on the table as soon as possible. When, as a salesperson, you ask for additional objections, make sure to ask the prospect if he likes everything else about your proposal. The implication of this question is that if you can answer your prospect's specific, tangible objections, then everything is good to go and he will buy what you are selling.

The last thing I want to highlight about the sample conversation is that when the salesperson asked his final question, he gave the prospect the opportunity to say that he likes the product, and at the same time, the prospect clarified the objection even more. Things mean more when they are said aloud. If you can get your prospect to say that he likes what you are pitching, you are that much closer to making the sale. This is because your prospect will, in some way, internalize what he hears himself saying.

Handling Objections

There are several ways to respond to objections, depending on what they are. If the objection is about understanding, meaning that the prospect is not sure about certain details of your product or service, then the key is to make sure you first clarify what is not understood. When you are answering objections, remember to keep all your explanations in simple, understandable terms, like you did during the initial sales pitch. Stay away from anything that will only lead to more confusion. If the objection is about value or price, make sure you explain the benefits received in exchange for the prospect's investment. In other words, look for ways to increase either perceived value or perceived need, as was discussed earlier.

Every product can be sold; it's just a matter of how hard you would need to work to increase the perceived need or value. Presumably, a salesperson who is so good that they can sell ice to an Eskimo has mastered the ability to demonstrate potential loss or potential gain to the point where his prospect would buy anything.

In the end, the Professional Salesperson knows that if his prospect does not accept his responses to the objections, that prospect is truly not ready to buy. The salesperson doesn't need to resort to sales tricks or closing techniques in order to get the deal signed. There are many reasons why a prospect doesn't buy from the salesperson in the end. The best thing a salesperson could do is listen to a prospect's current needs, and propose a solution that shows how whatever he is selling meets those needs. Sometimes, there's just not a good match.

I spoke earlier about the fact that sales is about competition. Personally, as a Professional Salesperson, I feel that there is nothing more rewarding than getting a signed contract, or getting a prospect to agree to the sale. However, an important part of sales is being able to handle rejection. Just like any competition, you win some and you lose some. Even as an Accidental Salesperson, I'm sure you don't always get your way. Professional Salespeople are guaranteed to face rejection everyday. They know that if they make cold calls, they're going to get hung up on. If they're giving a presentation, people are going to say *no*. It comes with the territory, so all salespeople try to accept it. All the salesperson can do is be a good listener and if his product or service can meet the needs of the prospect, he'll show them how. However, if, after all is said and done, his prospect still says *no* to the pitch, there's just one thing left to do—confirm why that prospect is not ready to agree to the sale and try to establish a time or condition that he can call back when the prospect would possibly buy.

Here is some sample dialogue, again going back to the Mail Wizard 1000, as an example of how to handle things when a prospect finally does say *no*. Assuming all other objections have been handled, but ...

PROSPECT: "I'm sorry, everything looks good, but I can't buy at this time."

SALESPERSON: "I'm sorry to hear that. That's OK. However, if you don't mind me asking, what is it that is preventing you from buying the product?"

PROSPECT: "It's just that we signed a lease for our current mail processor, and it won't expire for another five months."

SALESPERSON: "But you like everything else about the Mail Wizard?" [**Note: The salesperson is reconfirming that at this stage in the process, there is only one outstanding objection]

PROSPECT: "Absolutely. It would definitely help things run smoother around here, and it will save us a lot of money."

SALESPERSON: "Great. So, in other words, you agree that the Mail Wizard can help the business, and you are looking to implement it into your office as soon as your current lease expires?"

PROSPECT: "Yes."

There you have it. The salesperson has been able to get his prospect to confirm he likes the product, and that it would be a good addition to the business. The salesperson has also been able to confirm a time and condition under which the prospect will buy. At this point, all the salesperson would need to do is follow-up within the appropriate time frame.

The Accidental Salesperson Handles Objections

Just like the Professional Salesperson who handles objections on a daily basis, the Accidental Salesperson can use the same techniques to increase his chances of making the sale. Andrea is a great example of this. She is a mother of a five-year-old who constantly challenges her authority as a parent. Like most kids this age, Andrea's son wants what he wants, and typically won't accept "no" for an answer. However, even a four-year-old can be *sold* to.

The other day, Andrea was trying to get her son to finish his dinner. Of course, he wanted to skip dinner and get straight to dessert. It was time for Andrea, the Accidental Salesperson, to put sales skills into action. As I talked about in this chapter, the best way to handle objections is to allow the prospect, in this case, her son, to get all objections out on the table, rather than haggling over each objection one by one. Obviously, Andrea's son has several objections to finishing his dinner, but Andrea cannot simply accept his excuse of "I don't want my dinner." That objection is too vague. Andrea needs to get her son to express a more tangible objection:

ANDREA: "Tell Mommy why you don't want to eat your dinner."

ANDREA'S SON: "I don't like it."

ANDREA: "What don't you like?"

SON: "It's too hot."

ANDREA: "Is that all? Is there anything else you don't like?"

SON: "The pieces are too big. I can't eat the big pieces. I want you to cut it up."

All objections have now been made tangible and now she can go for the first attempt to get the "sale."

ANDREA: "That's it? If I make smaller pieces for you, and I cool the food down, will you eat your dinner?"

SON: "Yes."

Andrea just made a successful sale. She made sure to get all the objections out on the table and then confirmed the objections before answering. Once her son had admitted that those were his only two objections, Andrea could take the next steps of rectifying the problem by overcoming the objections and making the sale, which was getting her son to eat his dinner.

People Hate to Say "No"

If the example from the last chapter regarding the Professional Salesperson and the Mail Wizard 1000 was a real situation, I would say that the response the salesperson received was basically "we will buy your product in five months." So, the next logical sales step would be for the salesperson to draft up a purchase order for the prospect to sign where the order is not scheduled to be implemented for five months. This would just be another way to get additional confirmation of the prospect's intent and his readiness to accept the sales proposal. In the worst case scenario, this kind of action simply opens the door to another objection which the salesperson could then process.

The reason the salesperson should look to draft a purchase order in that case is because once something is in writing, it takes on a little more importance. Even if the salesperson is just creating a rough draft of a future agreement, by allowing the prospect to see his own written commitment, the salesperson is that much closer to making the sale. Car dealers do this kind of thing all the time. Have you ever noticed that if you walk into a dealership to look at cars, one of the first things that the salesperson will do is sit you down at a desk and start asking about the things you would like in your car? Not only do they ask you specifics, but they start *writing things down* on a sample purchase order.

Why go through all the extra effort? **People hate to say no to anything**. Because of this, all good salespeople try to get this extra level of commitment. Professional Salespeople have had plenty of experience giving what they thought was a great sales pitch, only to never hear from the prospect again. People hate to say no. They would much rather ignore the salesperson's phone calls and attempts to get in touch with them than say they are not interested.

For a real world example, think all the way back to high school. Did you ever ask someone out on a date and they responded with a flat-out *no*? Not likely. You probably got an answer like, "I'll have to check what I'm doing that day," or "I can't do it then," or "I'm getting my head shaved that day." These are all variations on the word that throws every salesperson, Accidental or Professional, off their game. That word is *maybe*. This is one of the worst words in the English language because it is so non-committal. In fact, it is probably the most non-committal word you could find in the dictionary. The word *maybe* gives false hope, it makes you waste your time, and it distracts you from your goal.

There is a reason why I continue to talk about the need for understanding throughout the sales process. By gaining mutual understanding, and most importantly confirmation, you can help to eliminate the waffling that a word like *maybe* would cause. How many times in your life did someone you were pitching give you a variation on the word *maybe*? It took an eternity for you to realize all of your time and effort that was wasted because of the false hope that your prospect gave you. Gaining understanding and confirmation by asking follow-up questions eliminates the negative elements of the word *maybe*.

It's perfectly acceptable to ask tough follow-up questions. I was talking about car salesmen earlier. They have a reputation for asking the question "What's it going to take to put you in this car?" That is actually a great follow-up question. Think about it—a question like that is an open invitation to mutual understanding between the salesperson and the prospect. If that question is answered honestly, then both parties will know exactly where they stand. Again, the prospect might not buy in the end, but at least everyone knows the ground rules for the potential sales exchange.

When the Professional Salesperson is on the front lines selling anything, he helps to avoid waffling by being more direct with his follow-up questions. Pretend, for the sake of example, it has been a while since the salesperson's last conversation with his prospect. If the prospect hasn't returned any phone calls, the salesperson might try something like this on his next attempt:

"I've left several messages that have gone unreturned. I know you're probably keeping busy, but I just wanted to follow-up to see if you are still interested in [my product/service]. If you're not, that's fine, please let me know and I will stop trying to reach you."

Or, it could be as simple as:

"It has been a while since we last spoke. You obviously have concerns about my product. Can we schedule a time to go over those issues?"

Some of the important points to notice with these two examples for phone conversations is that in the first suggestion, I added the line "... you're probably keeping busy." The fact is that they probably <u>are</u> keeping busy—we all keep busy. By making this statement, the salesperson is acknowledging that his prospect's time is important. This is just another way of showing respect. The second part of this quote, "... if you're not, that's fine," tries to alleviate the innate nature of people to not wanting to give a definitive "no." The Professional Salesperson will help the prospect understand that it is OK for them to give a clear negative answer. Granted, the prospect still may give the salesperson some kind of variation of *maybe*, but then again, the salesperson is just trying to increase his odds of getting to a resolution.

The second quote is just another way to try to get the issue resolved. In this quote, the salesperson is trying to reestablish the dialogue and rapport he had built during his earlier meetings. By saying "... you obviously have concerns ..." the salesperson should get one of two reactions:

1) "We don't have any concerns." This should prompt the salesperson to ask the logical follow-up question of "In that case, what obstacles are preventing you from buying my product?"

2) "You're right, I do have one major concern." This initiates the objection handling portion of the presentation again.

Throughout this part of the process, the Professional Salesperson will continue to focus on confirming all of the outstanding issues. After he gives a presentation, and maybe after some follow-up, he will be able to get either a "yes," meaning that he made the sale, or a "no," meaning that he didn't make the sale, but he can begin a relationship for follow-up which will help him get in position for success in the future.

Negotiation

The ability to negotiate is the single most important skill that a salesperson can have. This is for two reasons:

1) Negotiation is an essential part of the sales journey towards a mutually beneficial outcome.
2) Almost everything in life is negotiable.

I'm not claiming that you will be able to successfully negotiate for almost everything; it's just that *almost everything is negotiable.* In other words, regardless of the product or service, there is usually the possibility of negotiation between the buyer and seller. In reality, the reason that a negotiation doesn't take place for every transaction is because many times:

1) Either one of the people in the deal doesn't know that the option to negotiate is available.
2) Either party does not have the power to negotiate.
3) It's just that the product or service is simply too difficult to negotiate.

Most people know that the price of a car is negotiable, and that advertising rates are often negotiable, but did you know that you could negotiate for everything from mattresses to furniture, to haircuts?

In order to see the importance of negotiation in today's economy, think back to the origins of our economic system. In the beginning, before there was a standard monetary system, the way that goods and services were exchanged was through what is called *barter*. In general, the way it would work was that merchants would specialize in creating certain products, and then they would take these products to their neighbors for a potential exchange of the goods which each of them uniquely had. The key here was exchanging part of a finite supply of goods each seller had for goods he lacked. For example, the sheep herder would accumulate a supply of wool from his sheep. He had more wool than he knew what to do with, so he brought the surplus to the farmer next door. The farmer has an excess of corn from his crop, but he needs the wool to make clothing. The sheepherder needs corn for his food. Each of these parties has something that his counterpart needs, and each needed something that his counterpart has. At this point, they can start a negotiation. So, the two parties determine the relative value of wool to corn, and they make the exchange.

In a barter system, the value is inherently *subjective* based on supply and demand, as well as market conditions. In this case, are there any better offers? How hungry is the sheep herder? How desperate is the farmer for clothing? There might be other factors, like time of year, season, etc. In this example, the *sale* or transaction was completed without the use of a standardized monetary system. At the time, maybe a bushel of wool traded for 10 ears of corn. Maybe next week, for whatever reason, maybe it's getting closer to winter and the farmer needs more wool for a sweater, the bushel of wool will trade for 15 ears of corn. Again, the amount of goods that are traded and the value of what was being traded will be completely subjective. In this example, the farmer and the sheepherder *negotiated* until they settled on a mutually acceptable volume for the goods being exchanged.

Marketplaces grew out of this sort of early trade, as merchants from all over a geographical area would meet in one central place to exchange goods. However, even at these early marketplaces, the value of goods being traded remained subjective, following the basic economic principal of supply and demand.

The reason why almost everything is negotiable is because if you consider the two parties in the negotiation, one side of the sales interaction will typically have something that the other person does not, and vice versa. When negotiating today, keep in mind the nature of ancient marketplaces—many people bringing items of different value to a common place. These are the sales interactions you go through everyday.

A quick example of a situation where a negotiation could take place is the parent and child. For example, say your 12-year-old wants to go to the movies with his friends. He needs you to drive him. Your ability to drive the car has no specific monetary value, but it is your asset in the negotiation. So, the simple negotiation could be you, as the parent, and your child making a barter trade, which is a trade between two things that have no monetary value—if your child cleans up his room in the next hour, you'll take him to the movies.

From this point on, I will refer to all items being negotiated as *tradables*. Tradables are present in any negotiation, regardless of what is being negotiated. It's important that I refer to items being negotiated as tradables for two reasons:

1) You do not necessarily need to assign any monetary value to them.

2) In a negotiation, it is irrelevant whether the item being negotiated is a product or a service—it's simply an item being *traded*.

The main challenge with any sort of negotiation is getting the tradables out on the table. In other words, in order to conduct an effective negotiation, you have to know what all the potential tradables are, so that you will know the scope of the negotiation field. As a salesperson, as a buyer, or as anyone involved in the sales process, remember that you will typically have something that the other party does not, which means that you will typically own something which can be used to negotiate for something else.

Not all negotiations result in the win-win solution that we're looking for. The reason most negotiations fail is because the parties have not laid out all tradables. For a more detailed example of how a negotiation can happen and be successful without any money being exchanged, I will go back to a sports analogy. There was a trade that was listed in the newspaper a couple of weeks ago involving two football teams. One team traded its back-up quarterback in exchange for the other team's back-up running back and a second-round draft pick in next year's draft. This trade can be seen as a barter negotiation between the two teams for tradeables. In this case, football players.

Why would a team trade a quarterback for a running back when these two athletes had different skills that could not be quantified into a specific monetary amount? It all goes back to the resources each party had. It was a trade based on the different assumed value of each party's tradables. The two teams looked at their roster and examined their strengths and weaknesses. One team had a strong starting quarterback and a solid third-string quarterback, yet they didn't really have a great running back. The other team had a strong running back, but desperately needed a quarterback to lead the team. The result of this negotiation was a classic win-win as each team was able to make itself stronger overall by giving up excess resources in exchange for assets that they lacked.

Using Needs Analysis to Uncover Tradables

Just because I haven't mentioned *needs analysis* for several pages doesn't mean that it has lost importance. As stated earlier, the needs analysis of a prospect is the backbone of the entire sales process. Whether you are a Professional or Accidental Salesperson, the needs analysis will not only help you build a sales pitch with the greatest chance of success, but it will also serve to lay out potential tradables you can use towards the end of the sales process, when you enter the actual negotiation phase.

During your first conversations with your prospect, it will not be entirely obvious as to what the tradables are. A thorough needs analysis approach will always increase your chances for success, since you will be learning early on in the process about future tradables. It is always better to have too much information on a prospect than not enough. In some cases, before entering the negotiation phase of the sales process, you may need to go back to your notes from the needs analysis meetings, or any other meetings you may have had along the way. By talking with your prospect about his needs, it may uncover even more concerns, which might allow you to realize additional tradables which can be used during the eventual negotiation. As always, remember to ask open-ended questions which will help your prospect to answer questions in-depth.

I have a perfect example of using underlying tradables in a negotiation from when I was selling internet advertising at AOL. I was pitching a car dealership on a $200,000 advertising campaign. I had finished what I thought was a strong sales presentation by showing how the advertising placements I was offering would help the dealership group get in front of their target audience, and how the focused advertising would help increase sales to the customers they wanted to bring in the door. However, we were still far apart on price—the dealership President thought I was about $25,000 too high. Following the process I had talked about before, I followed through to make sure that price was the only objection. In other words, I wanted to make sure that they liked everything about the proposal, assuming that price wasn't an issue. After it was confirmed that price was the only outstanding issue, we entered the negotiation stage of the sales process.

Overall, the dealership group thought the advertising campaign was too expensive, but I wasn't going to budge on price. After all, I had a sales quota to make, so I wasn't about to let a $200,000 deal fall to a $175,000 deal or worse. So, I went back to my notes from the previous two needs analysis meetings with the decisionmakers.

One side note is that I had to go through two needs analysis meetings for this partic-
ular prospect. I have found that, especially if you are a Professional Salesperson, in cases
where you are dealing with a more complex sale, you may need to go through multiple
needs analysis meetings. If there are several people involved in the final decision, this
would naturally take more time. Each person participating in the final decision brings
a different perspective to the table, and as a result, they may express different needs
than their peers. Before putting a sales pitch together, make sure you have completed a
needs analysis with every one of the decision makers involved. Even for the Accidental
Salesperson, like the teenager trying to get his parents to allow him to get a later curfew,
if both parents are equally involved in the decision, he should make sure to have needs
analysis information relevant to both of those decision makers.

In the case concerning the car dealership, I looked back at my needs analysis
notes and saw that in one of the meetings, the President had mentioned that his
sales staff was not comfortable using the internet and that before he would consider internet advertising, he was going to look into sending his salespeople to an
Internet 101 class so they could learn computer basics, e-mail functionality, etc.
During that meeting, I asked him how much he thought it might cost to send
his salespeople to these training classes. It seemed like a fairly innocuous question
at the time, but I was now glad I had asked it, because that had given me more
ammunition for the present negotiation. Remember, when you are conducting a
needs analysis, it's always better to have more information than not enough—ask
any question that comes to your mind, since you never know when the prospect
will give you information you could use later. In my situation, the President said
that for some of the series of classes he had looked at, it would cost in the neigh-
borhood of $50,000 to $70,000 to get his sales staff up-to-speed.

At the time, I had been selling internet advertising for over 5 years, which was
considered a lifetime of experience to anyone out of the industry. Of course, I now
know that today, there are probably kids in grade school that know more about
computers than I do, but in the late nineties, internet knowledge as it applied to
business was at a premium. So, because of my experience in the internet industry,
and my experience working with other businesses to build successful advertising
campaigns, as well as the knowledge I had picked up over the years by working
on the front lines of the internet revolution, I felt I could offer some value to my
prospect. I thought a little bit out-of-the-box and realized that I had a valuable
tradable I had not considered in the first place. Soon, I had all of the tradables out
on the table.

Here is a listing of the tradables, with consideration for the two parties, which we started with:

MY TRADABLES	DEALERSHIP'S TRADABLES
Advertising space ($200,000)	$175,000**

*** They thought we were overpriced by $25,000, so this means that they were only willing to "trade" $175,000 in cash for the advertising.*

Money can, of course, be a tradable. It is something that one party gives to another in exchange for goods and services. However, looking at the original scenario, the sales proposal seemed a little too cut and dry, and we still had not reached an agreement.

This is a reason why most negotiations fail—people don't look past the original tradables. By digging a little deeper, and then referencing my notes from the needs analysis phase of the discussion, I was able to open up the negotiations by presenting additional tradables. After considering the idea of having me train their sales staff on computer basics, our chart of tradables now looked like this:

MY TRADABLES	DEALERSHIP'S TRADABLES
Advertising space ($200,000)	$175,000
Basic Internet Training (free)	$50,000**

*** $50,000 is the tradable for the sales training since the dealership said that an internet training class would cost at least this much.*

In other words, based on their expressed needs, the auto dealership was willing to pay $225,000 and receive advertising space on certain websites as well as send all their sales people to basic internet training class. $175,000 for advertising plus $50,000 for training.

I pitched the idea of having the President allow me to train their staff as a supplement to the advertising. However, in order to prove my worth, I said that I would meet for one hour with any two salespeople he wanted me to, and I would teach them some internet basics. We agreed that if the two salespeople he chose thought I knew what I was talking about and that I offered strong value to those employees, then I would be allowed to teach the whole staff. In the end, the dealership signed the $200,000 contract for the advertising I initially proposed to them, and I agreed to spend one hour a week at each of their dealerships training their salespeople on internet basics. So, I got what I wanted, a $200,000 contract, and the dealership saved $45,000, yet still got what they wanted, internet advertising and internet training. In addition, because I spent time at the dealership working with their sales staff, I was further able to strengthen the bond between me and my customers. This led to future sales opportunities with even bigger contract values. Remember how important the relationship is in sales—people buy from those they know, like, and trust.

Like the analogy I made earlier regarding the trade between two football teams, the example of the car dealership highlights another important lesson in negotiating—focus on a win/win solution. I once heard that "a good compromise leaves everybody angry." That's the main difference between a *compromise* and the outcome of a *negotiation*. A compromise assumes that both parties need to give in a little from their opening demands, and then end up with less than they had hoped for. However, you can have a successful negotiation without either party feeling that they gave something up unwillingly. It's all a matter of widening the scope of the negotiation by introducing as many tradables as possible. Regardless of the specific negotiation, it will always help to make sure that all issues are out on the table. When the Accidental Salesperson is in a situation with the potential for negotiation, he should try to think what issues are of value to his prospect, and then start looking for out-of-the-box solutions.

The key to finding additional tradables is by conducting a thorough needs analysis and referencing the notes from that meeting, or meetings. During the needs analysis phase, the salesperson is more likely to get information which will deliver future benefits because it is early in the sales process. Using the example above, if, during the needs analysis meetings, I had not been able to get the decisionmaker to tell me he was looking into sales training, along with what it costs, I am sure that he would not have given that information up towards the end of the sales process, and I wouldn't have had the benefit of that valuable tradable later in the sales process.

As we talked about earlier, confidence is an important part of the sales pitch. Along these same lines, assertiveness is an important part of the negotiation phase of the sales process. Actually, these two elements, confidence and assertiveness, go hand in hand throughout an effective negotiation. The bottom line is that **if you don't ask for something, you'll never get it.** Also, if you don't have the confidence that your product or service can benefit your prospect, you're not going to sell anything.

Assertiveness is a great tool that the Accidental Salesperson can use to quickly get a leg-up during a negotiation. Being assertive can also help to uncover tradables that neither party knew existed. Take this sample dialogue between a homeowner and a painter. In this example, we're joining in the middle of the negotiation. The painter has already given his price which the homeowner feels is a little too high. The painter has said that it will take him at least a week to get the job done. Even though this is acceptable to the homeowner, he decides to be assertive in an effort to try to get a better deal. Here's a sample dialogue:

> HOMEOWNER: "Is there any way you come down a little on the price?"

> PAINTER: "I'm sorry. I can't lower the price. Actually, the job is only going to take three days, so I'm only charging you for three days of work. The reason I said it would take a week to finish is because after tomorrow, I'm going away for a couple days on a golf trip."

> HOMEOWNER: "I didn't know you golfed. My cousin is a golf pro at the club down the street. If I could get him to give you some free lessons next month, could you take a little bit off the price?"

The painter, seeing that the cost of golf lessons will be more than a couple hours of labor costs for painting, agrees.

Of course, this example is completely oversimplified, but the point is that many things in life are open for negotiation.

Another important consideration in negotiations is making sure that you are dealing with someone who has the power to negotiate the sale. This is why it is easier to negotiate with a painter, as in the example above, since he is probably the business owner, than one employee of an international corporation. This is also the main reason why you rarely can negotiate for anything at the huge superstores like Target or Wal-Mart. In these cases, the cashier at the check-out counter has not been empowered to make barter deals for the merchandise, or even to discount the pricing.

> In order to truly have an effective negotiation, both parties in the discussion need to have the ability and resources to introduce tradables that can be exchanged.

If we look again at the trade between two football teams, that trade could not have taken place if, for example, a cheerleader on one team was discussing options with the punter on the other team. The reason being that neither of these two parties in the negotiation actually had the power to dictate changes in the composition of the team. That responsibility would most likely be reserved for the General Manager, Director of Scouting, and/or a Vice President of Operations.

Identifying the principal players in a negotiation is much like prospecting, where the actual job title isn't important—job *responsibility* is. Regardless of what someone puts on their business card, the important factor to take into account is whether or not the people involved in the negotiation have the ability to offer tradables which will help bring about a satisfactory resolution.

Earlier in the book, I talked about the importance of relationship-building when dealing with sales prospects. Another reason to make sure that your negotiations end in a win/win situation is that if the negotiations lead to you making a sale, you will most likely have an ongoing relationship with the prospect. Think about the example of the homeowner and the painter. Even after that job is completed, both parties still need the relationship to be on good terms. The homeowner may need another room painted in the future and the painter may need referrals for other jobs.

Even if your negotiation does not result in a sale, you want to make sure that the negotiation still ends with both sides happy. In this respect, all sales interactions should be the same—the salesperson conducts the needs analysis meeting for a reason—he's trying to have an open discussion with the prospect so that he can learn how the product or service he is pitching can have a positive impact on the prospect. For the Professional Salesperson, if he doesn't think that his product or service can benefit the prospect, or if he doesn't truly care about the person or business he is pitching, he will probably consider moving on to the next prospect.

Moving on isn't a bad thing. As we talked about earlier, sales success is built on a foundation of planning which leads to efficiency. The Professional Salesperson knows to not waste his time meeting with businesses which aren't a good fit for what he is selling. Similarly, as the Accidental Salesperson, if you progress through a negotiation and you just can't get to a sale, or a positive resolution to the negotiation, you can end the sales interaction amicably. Just focus on follow-up and keep building the relationship for another time.

The Accidental Salesperson Negotiates a Deal

My father taught me my first lessons in the art of negotiation. He's a doctor by trade, but definitely a great example of an Accidental Salesperson. As I mentioned earlier in the book, there are thousands of things that can be negotiated, especially the final sales price of a new car. It was the times my Dad went to buy new cars that he shined as a negotiator. My father did everything that should be expected of an Accidental Salesperson preparing to initiate a negotiation:

1. He did his research beforehand.
2. He was able to get all tradables out on the table.
3. He wasn't afraid to walk away from the deal.

The best example I have of my father negotiating for a new car was over fifteen years ago, when I went with him to a dealership. Back then, the internet wasn't as popular as it is today, and you couldn't just log onto Edmunds.com to get the invoice price of a car versus what the dealer pays for it, etc. In order to do effective research back then, you needed to get your hands on the Kelly Blue Book. So, before Dad even set foot in a dealership, he researched the different features and advantages of the different cars he was going to choose from. Then, he finalized his target.

In this case, the invoice price on the car he was looking to buy was $17,100. We went into the dealership and were greeted by a salesperson who listened to us, and then finally sat us down at his desk to build out a pricing sheet. I don't remember exactly, but the salesperson's first run through the pricing sheet came up at over $19,500. This was not what Dad was looking for.

This is when my Dad started to let the salesperson know there were additional tradables other than cash available. He asked if there were any incentives available on buying the car. Of course, he knew there were incentives from his research, but at this stage of the negotiation, the Accidental Salesperson needs to get all tradables out on the table.

After more negotiating, the price was now down to $17,900. Dad still held firm asking to pay the invoice price.

*[**NOTE: This is an important negotiation technique that a lot of professional salespeople use—hold firm on your position for as long as possible.]*

The salesperson said that he was not authorized to bring the price any lower, he would need to get his manager. Remember what I was talking about earlier— when negotiating, you want to deal with the person who is empowered to negotiate and make a decision. After about 15 minutes, we were escorted up to the sales manager's office. The sales manager said he could bring the price down to $17,700, but that was as far as he could go. Then, Dad put his research to work again:

"Thank you for giving us the incentive discount, but doesn't the dealership get a bonus for selling a certain number of cars? Also, we both know it's costing you money to keep the car on the lot. I'm willing to come up to $17,300. I'll buy the car right now and this will help you reach your monthly sales bonus."

The sales manager now fully realized that he was dealing with an educated customer. The rest of the negotiation played out successfully for us, but it wouldn't have if the Accidental Salesperson wasn't willing to walk away. After my Dad raised his asking price to $17,300, and after leaving the office for another fifteen minutes, the sales manager responded:

> SALES MANAGER: "I looked through everything, and I can give a final price of $17,600."

> DAD: "I'm looking to pay $17,300 for this car. Thank you for your time, however I'm going to need to go to another dealership."

> SALES MANAGER: "But you're here now. Are you really going to walk over $300?"

> DAD: "Are you really going to let me walk over $300?"

End of negotiation. Dad bought the car for $17,300.

After the "No" or After the Sale

After the "No"

Another important part of the sales process comes after the initial sales pitch. For most salespeople, the one-call close, which means making the sale during the very first interaction with the prospect, is rare. Anything outside of the one-call close involves persistent but polite follow-up. The Professional Salesperson will make sure to stay in touch with his prospect throughout each step of the sales process.

> Regardless of what you are selling, regardless of whether you are an Accidental or Professional Salesperson, follow-up is what separates a good salesperson from a great salesperson.

I continue to be amazed at how this simple aspect of sales is so easily forgotten, but it is rare for a prospect to be so excited about any product that he initiates the call back to the salesperson, asking to buy. Most sales are made after the salesperson follows-up from the initial pitch.

I have even come across plenty of examples of poor follow-up in my everyday life. About six months ago, I wanted to buy a new car. I sent e-mails to five different dealerships. Only three dealerships even responded to that initial e-mail. I went into those three dealerships to see the cars and only two of those called me back to see if I was still interested. The lack of follow-up eliminated 60% of the dealerships from making the sale.

I see examples of poor follow-up in the business world every day. As recently as two months ago, my colleague and I were looking into joining a trade association. The Membership Director gave us her pitch and we left the meeting asking her for referrals of current members we could talk with in order to learn more about their experience with the group. No only did we not hear back from the Membership Director, but I had to leave three messages over two weeks asking again for the names of references we could call. All she needed to do was follow-up, and she probably would have gotten our business. It is amazing how many sales people miss this step. The most important thing to remember after giving a sales pitch is that most of the time, you will not get the sale if you don't follow-up.

The goal of a Professional Salesperson's follow-up interaction will typically be to maintain contact with his prospect in order to make sure that he can remain top-of-mind with that business as he continues to work toward his goal of making the sale. This goes back to the continued effort to build the relationship. Most prospects will appreciate responsible follow-up that delivers value to them personally or to their business.

I have said that when a Professional Salesperson gives his sales pitch, there are a variety of factors that go into his prospect's overall decision-making process. Also, the Professional Salesperson will remember that small changes in any of these factors can have a huge impact on that business or individual, and thus, will impact whether or not a sale is made. Depending on the nature of the particular sales interaction, the salesperson will try to develop a way to stay in touch with his prospect, and make sure that each subsequent interaction delivers value to the prospect by referencing one of the many factors that may be affecting him. By doing this, the salesperson will be highlighting his understanding of the prospect's needs and the prospect's business, as well as his dedication to his prospect's success. Again, this is a great way for follow-up to serve as a way to build a relationship.

The Professional Salesperson's method of follow-up and the information that he provides for follow-up will vary greatly depending on the industry he is involved in, as well as each specific sales situation. A great tool that Professional Salespeople use for follow-up is a company newsletter or similar e-mail communication. In the age of e-mail, this not only serves as an efficient way for the salesperson to easily get in touch with many of prospects and customers, but since they don't need to pay for postage, it is extremely cost-efficient. Successful salespeople will look to create an e-mail newsletter not only for their existing clients, or people they've worked with in the past, but also for their prospects. This helps to position the salesperson and the business he is representing as a trusted source in his field. If the salesperson is respected as a trusted source, or someone who knows what they're talking about, then the prospect is more likely to buy.

People buy from those they know, like, and trust.

Trust and relationship-building are important parts of selling. In fact, in the end, most sales are about trust. The prospect is taking a leap of faith that the product or service the salesperson is offering will actually meet his expressed needs. I can't say it enough—**trust is important** because people buy from those they know, like, and trust.

When a prospect says "no" to whatever you're pitching, more often than not, it actually means "not now." In other words, when you hear the word *no* from a prospect, it usually means that there is something in the current environment that is preventing him from accepting your proposal. It may have to do with money, or it may have to do with the lack of urgency of his need. This is why follow-up is so important—you never know when those factors may change.

Here's an exercise that professional salespeople use to help with follow-up. There might be some aspects of the exercise you could apply to your life as the Accidental Salesperson. The Professional Salesperson will pull out his calendar and look back one month. Then, he'll write down the names and phone numbers of all the people that he pitched during that month. For the Accidental Salesperson, this could include the painter, the car dealer, the mortgage banker, your kids, etc. Continuing the exercise, the Professional Salesperson will then look back at his calendar from three months ago and do the same thing. He now has a list of people that he pitched one month ago, and people that he pitched three months ago. From that list of names, the Professional Salesperson will separate the people who were "sold" on whatever was being pitched.

The final step in this exercise is that the salesperson will pull out the list of people who he gave a pitch to, but who didn't buy, and get back in touch with every one of them. When he contacts them, his goal is to find the answers to these two questions:

1) Why didn't that prospect buy from him in the past? In the case of the Accidental Salesperson, the question would be, "Why did the sales pitch fail?"

2) Is there an opportunity for the salesperson to pitch to that prospect again?

If the answer to the second question is "no," then the salesperson will most likely just ask if it would be OK for him to re-contact that prospect in three months just to check in. Even if someone is saying no to the salesperson in terms of not buying what he is selling, it would be rare for the prospect to forbid the salesperson from ever following-up again.

> Follow-up is about being there for the prospect when they need you, even if that doesn't mean *right now*.

There can really only be good things that can come out of the kind of follow-up interaction I just described. More likely than not, the prospect will appreciate the follow-up, since it shows that the salesperson was thinking about him—that is flattering to anyone.

The two big reasons Professional Salespeople use an exercise like I just described to improve their follow-up skills is because it allows them to separate themselves from their peers in a good way. Unfortunately, most salespeople don't follow-up. Remember the old adage *the squeaky wheel gets the oil*. A good salesperson knows he can never assume that the prospect will get back in touch when he is ready to buy. This is why successful salespeople follow-up. They know that sales are rarely made at the first contact. It's typically the 3rd, 4th, 5th, or even longer. The other benefit of this kind of exercise is that the salesperson will no doubt get some new appointments from this batch of calls, as well as some great feedback that he may use to optimize his sales pitch in the future.

In any kind of business, big or small, or even with individuals, things change all the time. Many times I've called someone back after not speaking to him for three months to find that he no longer works at the company, or that maybe there was someone else responsible for making the decision on whatever I was selling. Or maybe, things have changed at that business in the last three months that now my product would actually be a perfect fit for the prospect's needs. It's always good to touch base with people even after they have said "no" to the initial sales pitch because you never know how their environment may have changed.

Now back to the exercise—at this point, the Professional Salesperson has covered one important part of the sales process—follow-up. Continuing with the exercise, after the salesperson completes the calls on the list of people who rejected him one or three months ago, he will pull out the second list, the one with the people who have bought from him. A great thing the Professional Salesperson would do here is to call them back and simply check-in. Basically, get a status report. He'll ask the customer if he is happy with whatever he had sold them. If the customer isn't happy, he'll talk to the appropriate person about how to resolve the problem, and then take care of it. The customer will appreciate the fact that the salesperson is taking responsibility for his sale and that he is working to resolve the problem quickly. If, when the salesperson calls his client, he finds out that that person is happy with the product or service, he'll move the conversation towards referrals. By doing this correctly, the salesperson will find he will get at least one referral from each prospect. Think about it—the client has just said they think that they have bought a good product, or that they are happy with the service which the salesperson has provided. How could that client then turn around and say that what the salesperson is selling would not be good for anyone else? On the other side of the coin, if and when a prospect says "no" to your sales pitch, it may help for you to ask the question "What are the main reasons that you are not interested in [whatever I'm selling] at this time?" Those last three words are so important because you are getting your prospect to think about a time when he would be sold on what you are pitching, and you are leaving the door open for a future relationship. A great follow-up to whatever their answer is would be, "So, although I do not have this [element(s)] at this time, would you be ready to work with me if I did?" Again, the goal is to try to get close to a black and white explanation of the conditions under which the prospect would buy.

It's easy to come up with examples of how this can be applied to the Accidental Salesperson. Think back to the example of the teenager who was trying to convince his parents to loan him the car for the night. After all possibilities have been exhausted, and his parents still say "no," the last question he should ask is, "Why won't you let me borrow the car *tonight*?" This question will force his parents to give a tangible explanation as to why his sales pitch wasn't successful. Maybe their response could be something as simple as "You can't borrow the car tonight because it just snowed last night and we're worried about you driving on the icy roads. If the weather clears-up, you can borrow the car next weekend." In that case, the Accidental Salesperson now knows the conditions under which his sales pitch will be successful.

After the Sale

If you have made a successful pitch, you have probably done a great needs analysis, given a strong presentation which showed how your product or service meets the needs of your prospect and would deliver value to him, and you have reached a mutual agreement. Congratulations! You have made the sale.

The diligence and persistence you showed when chasing after that sale should continue to be present after the sale as well. For the Professional Salesperson, he has worked so hard to bring the new client on board; he won't want to lose this golden opportunity to develop his business even further. Every Professional Salesperson knows that the easiest sale is a referral, and overall, his current customers should be a breeding ground for an exponential increase in sales. Depending on what the Professional Salesperson is selling, there may be a chance for renewal of the current sale, if, for example, he is selling advertising to a small business on short-term contracts. At the very least, there is the opportunity for the salesperson to expand his business based on the client he has just sold to. When a client is happy with his product or service, the Professional Salesperson asks for a referral. He can even do this immediately after making the sale.

Follow-up after the sale is easily applicable in the world of the Accidental Salesperson. Earlier, I gave the example of fundraising. In that scenario, a successful sale is getting someone to donate money. Immediately after the sale, it would not be unreasonable for the fundraiser to ask the new donor, "Do you know of anyone else who might be interested in helping the cause?" Even if you, as the Accidental Salesperson, are in a situation where you can't immediately ask for a referral, you should start laying the groundwork as soon as you get the opportunity.

Several chapters ago I talked about trackability and accountability. At the time, I was referring to building a prospecting list and tracking the success of an outbound sales effort, but the same documentation can and should be used to build on your success after the sale. Again, the key is to develop a process and identify metrics for success. Ask yourself:

"What do I do with this prospect after I've made the sale?"

There are thousands of different ways that the Professional Salesperson has devised to stay in touch with his current clients and build his business. Maybe he'll send a personalized thank-you note after a new client signs up. He might try sending flowers or even just stopping by the client's office a month or so after he made the sale. If that salesperson has a documented history of successful follow-up after his sales, he will be able to repeat his success in order to get more business.

One of the most important things to remember is that as a salesperson, your work does not end after the sale is made. Look back to the example of Tom, the Accidental Salesperson who is a painter. Even if he were to make the successful *sale* of finding someone who will let him paint the house, he shouldn't stop there. The relationship is important before, during, and after the sale. **People buy from who they know, like, and trust, and** *people give referrals to people they know, like and trust.* Tom will let his current clients know that he looks to build business through referrals. Sometimes, this is all it takes to get clients to start thinking of people who the salesperson could sell to. In fact, even as the Accidental Salesperson, regardless of the prospect you are pitching to, make sure that as many people as possible know that you aim to build your business through referrals. This will help you get more leads. The Professional Salesperson is always mindful of the "six degrees of separation" rule—in other words; everyone is connected to everyone else within six steps. For example, even though the salesperson's dry cleaner, for example, might not be a perfect client, that dry cleaner may know someone who knows someone who just might buy from the salesperson. The Professional Salesperson will let his current customers know what types of businesses he is calling on—not only are happy customers his best sources of referrals, but his customers certainly know other businesses that could benefit from the salesperson's product or service. This is a great reason to have a strong value proposition nailed down. The salesperson always needs to be able to tell anyone he meets what his product or service can do.

I've already talked about the fact that trust and relationship-building play a key role in all sales. Another fact about sales prospects, big or small, is that they like to know what other people like themselves are doing. Referral letters, or just points of reference that you can describe to your prospects, offer some comfort. Remember back to the fact that if you could optimize your time and make any part of the sales process more efficient, you will be in a better position. If a referral gets you closer to your goal of making the sale, it's simply a more efficient use of your time.

Getting referrals should be a natural part of the sales process. If a salesperson sells someone a product or service which meets that person's needs, then the salesperson has done everything he can on the front end of the sale. If his customers can attest to the positive impact that his sale has had on their business, they should be more than willing to tell other people.

The Professional Salesperson will make sure that the relationship between him and his client is not one-sided. Within his network, chances are that the salesperson's prospects, and now clients, are also looking for referrals. If he can help his clients to build relationships with other people in the community, they will most likely do the same for him.

Here's a tip about referrals from professional salespeople which shows the importance of continued follow-up at all points in the relationship. If the salesperson pitches a product or service that is based on short term contracts, for example, a 3-month advertising campaign, they will ask for the renewal halfway through the current contract. There are two important things that could come out of this kind of initiative:

1) The customer will renew early, in which case the salesperson has an open door to ask for referrals. I would say something along the lines of, "As you can see, this advertising campaign worked so well for you, do you know of any other people or businesses that could have similar success?"

2) The customer could say that the performance of the ad campaign, for example, to date has not been successful enough to warrant an early renewal. In this case, the salesperson will discuss with the client the specific metrics which they are using to determine the success and current failure of the campaign. In other words, the salesperson will be able to essentially say to the prospect, "If we hit the metrics that you have defined, then would you consider this a successful campaign?"

The concept of referrals is just another part of building the relationship with your new client. Also, it's a way to help make your life easier as a salesperson.

Using e-mail

The successful Professional Salesperson is a master of technology. As discussed earlier, he will use the internet extensively as a resource tool, and he knows how to use e-mail to his advantage. As an Accidental Salesperson, you also have the benefit of e-mail, where you can communicate with prospects and clients instantaneously. I remember working at an ad agency when the fax machine was a novelty. I was so amazed that I could send graphical prints to another business over a simple phone line. My clients on the other end of the line would be able to see the mock-up almost immediately, as opposed to having to drop the proofs in the mail and wait two days for them to receive everything. Now, with e-mail, communication has been made even more instantaneous. The fax machine facilitated communication twenty years ago but now, the e-mail revolution has not only made it even easier to relay information between businesses, but can also serve as a valuable sales tool.

The fact that you can send information quickly through e-mail brings up an important point to keep in mind: **what you write in an e-mail can sometimes hold as much importance as a signed contract**. You should not only be prepared to communicate just as effectively through e-mail as you would in person, but you also need to respect the importance of e-mail as a component of the tools you can use as a salesperson. If you are sending e-mail to a sales prospect, remember to clean it up, and make sure that you mean exactly what you type. This includes proofreading. You would be surprised as to how many business e-mails I have seen where there are not only grammatical errors, but plenty of typos. Every e-mail communication you have with a future or current business partner should be checked and rechecked. In today's business world, e-mails can hold the same importance as a note printed on company letterhead. Respect the e-mail medium. Proofread your e-mails before you send them. Don't use slang or *instant message* abbreviations in business e-mails.

E-mail is a valuable tool in all interpersonal interactions. I've used the power of e-mail many times as a way to hold people to service obligations, since it's always best to get things in writing. For example, when my wife and I got a quote for a patio we were looking at, I made sure to send an e-mail to the contractor confirming the price that he had given me during our face-to-face meeting. I made sure that he confirmed the exact conditions of that proposal, how long the offer was good for, did we need to pay anything extra, etc. This way, if he tried to change the terms, I had something in writing to use as a reference point.

For the Professional Salesperson, response time of the e-mail becomes an important factor. E-mails are sent instantaneously. Whether it's fair or not, in a business environment, people expect a quicker response time when it comes to e-mails. There should be no reason why the Professional Salesperson does not respond to an e-mail within 24 hours. At the very least, he will let the sender know that he will be getting back in touch within a specific time frame.

Professional Salespeople will send prospects e-mails all the time. Sometimes, the prospect replies back with a question. If the salesperson doesn't know the answer to a question posed in an e-mail, or if he doesn't have the information that the sender requested, the salesperson will let that prospect know a specific time that he will get back with a response. This is not only a subtle show of respect to the prospect, but it may give the salesperson a leg-up on his sales competition. The Professional Salesperson knows what he is competing against—his peers are sending out e-mails with grammatical errors and they are forgetting to follow-up on them.

The Accidental Salesperson After the Sale or After the "No"

Going back to the example of Dan successfully negotiating the opportunity to take the car out, we can learn how the Accidental Salesperson responds after the sale. In Dan's case, the sale was made when his parents allowed him to take the car. However, just like with a Professional Salesperson, his job is not done as soon as the sale is made.

First of all, he needs to live up to the expectations and promises that he made during his sales presentation, like filling the tank up with gas at the end of the night. Also, he remembers that one of the concerns his parents had was whether or not he was responsible enough to take the car out for the night. So, in the days and weeks that follow, Dan goes out of his way to solidify his image as a responsible teenager in the eyes of his parents. He does extra chores, he even volunteers to pick up the weekly groceries for his mother. This kills two birds with one stone, since he is not only proving his ability to take care of household chores, but since he needs the car to get to the store, he's also proving that he can be trusted with the keys.

Continued follow-up after the sale can only deliver positive benefits for the salesperson and his clients.

Conclusion

I've covered a variety of concepts in this book, and I understand it might be a case of information overload. However, as I talked about in the beginning of the book, each person who reads this should pull out specific parts that he finds personally most applicable to himself. However, just to give you a 30-second summary, everything in this book can be boiled down into these five things you should remember:

1. *Salespeople are everywhere, and you run across sales situations every day of your life.*

   You've been a salesperson almost from the day you were born, and you've probably been using sales techniques in many of those interactions. By learning to identify sales situations, you will be able to achieve greater success in your efforts as the Accidental Salesperson.

2. *Preparation and confidence leads to sales success.*

   One of the most important elements of sales success is learning as much as you can about your prospect. The more you know about your prospect and his needs, the easier it will be for you to find a sales solution that both of you will agree upon.

   Also, never try to sell something that you don't believe will benefit your prospect. If you honestly believe that your product, service, or whatever you're pitching can help your prospect, then you will be more confident in your presentation. Your increased confidence makes it more likely that your prospect will feel comfortable accepting your sales proposal.

3. *Track your efforts and you'll work more efficiently.*

We all complain that there aren't enough hours in the day. One way to get back some of that time is to be more efficient. *If you're more efficient, you'll have more time to be successful.* The best way to maximize your efficiency in both the short-term and the long-term is to track your efforts. This will not only help you figure out where you may be wasting time, but as a salesperson, it will give you a historical record of what has worked for you in the past. This way, you won't make the same mistake twice.

4. *Every successful sales interaction should lead to a mutually beneficial result.*

A sales interaction is not successful if both parties are not truly gaining something from the relationship. For example, if you bring your clothes to be dry-cleaned, that's a successful sales interaction since both you and your dry cleaner are gaining something—you're getting clean clothes and he's getting paid. Other gains in sales interactions can be just as simple, or they may be more difficult to uncover. Remember that people buy from who they know, like, and trust. If you focus on making sure all of your sales interactions benefit all parties involved, you're going to be more successful in the long-term.

5. *Follow-up. Follow-up. Follow-up.*

Easy sales are lost all of the time simply because the salesperson doesn't follow-up. Out of sight, out of mind. You can't expect your prospect to make the next move. The bottom line is that if you want something, follow-up until you get a definitive resolution. If you honestly believe that whatever you are selling will help the prospect, you owe it to him, and yourself, to follow-up until you get a "yes" or "no."

It would be impossible to apply all of the concepts in this book into your life as an Accidental Salesperson, but you will find that there is a time and place to utilize many of the ideas that were covered. In fact, you might want to skim back through the book and just pick out one thing that you will take into your daily sales life.

I'll even get you started with one. Let's say that, after reading through this book once, and then skimming through it again, you have decided that the one concept that you would like to take into your life as the Accidental Salesperson is that you want to be more efficient. By the way, this would be a good choice, since efficiency typically leads to success. No matter what line of work you are in, if you can find a way to be more efficient, you will be better off.

Here's an exercise in efficiency for the Accidental Salesperson, which also covers concepts of planning and preparation. The point of the exercise is just to find more time in your day to do extra things.

So, the first step is to get a hold on how you spend your day. Tomorrow, just write down everything you do when you do it. You don't need to write down every tiny detail, but make sure that all of your time is accounted for. Include the time that you had breakfast, from the time you got into the kitchen, to the time the dishes were put away. Include the time it took you to go to the grocery store, starting with the time your car leaves the garage to the time you get back home. Put in any notes as to why things may have taken longer than you initially thought. Maybe it took 90 minutes at the grocery store because you didn't make a list beforehand and you were forced to walk up and down every aisle trying to remember what you needed to buy. Put in how long it took you to give your kids a bath, and then how long it took to put them to bed.

Do this exercise for a full week. Track everything that you do.

Then, at the end of the week, spread out the charts in front of you and critique yourself. Many times, you will find that it is easier to see inefficiencies when everything is laid out in front of you. Be honest with yourself and look for ways to become more efficient. You'll find little time savings that add up in the long run. For example, maybe by spending 10 minutes building a shopping list, you save 30 minutes in the grocery store. Your net savings are 20 minutes. Maybe if you leave your house 15 minutes earlier in the morning, you'll miss the rush-hour crunch and cut your commute by 25 minutes. That's over four hours per week!

There are exercises that you could create around every major concept in this book, and I go over additional examples during my sales seminars. Take the time to review your current sales efforts and then determine which concept will deliver the most immediate impact on your daily life. I have broken out the chapters into the different phases that you would encounter throughout the sales process, so my recommendation would be for you to reference each chapter depending on what stage you are at.

Happy selling!

Keep in Touch!

Send examples of your own Accidental Salesperson experiences.

You can send your stories through the website:
www.theaccidentalsalesperson.com

I'd love to hear from you!

978-0-595-45277-4
0-595-45277-9

Printed in the United States
90797LV00004B/307-324/A